To Paul,

Love,

Jennifer

Christmas 1986

ENGLISH COUNTRY PUBS

ENGLISH COUNTRY PUBS

Derry Brabbs

LITTLE, BROWN AND COMPANY

Boston Toronto

Library of Congress catalog card no. 85–82373

First American edition

First published in Great Britain in 1986

Designed by Helen Lewis

Half Title Page The Crown
Abbots Bromley, Staffordshire
Title Page The Bat and Ball
Hambledon, Hampshire

Printed and bound in Italy

CONTENTS

INTRODUCTION

The origins of the English pub probably lie in the Roman *tabernae vinariae*, small shops where wine and food were served to customers seated on stools around a communal table. But the oldest extant pubs in England date back to about the eleventh century, like the Cat and Fiddle at Hinton Admiral in Hampshire, or The Church House at Rattery in Devon. The claim to being the oldest pub in England is hotly disputed, but the most likely contenders to this title are pubs that can trace their origins to the hospices set up by monks to accommodate travellers and pilgrims on their way to recognized shrines. The Cat and Fiddle for instance, which offered shelter and refuge to travellers in the New Forest, was run by the monks of nearby Christchurch Priory, while medieval pilgrims visiting Glastonbury Abbey could stay at the George and Pilgrim, and those on their way to the shrine of St Richard at Chichester might put up at The Star Inn at Alfriston, a hospice owned by the monks of Battle Abbey.

This book is a personal selection of country pubs, it is not intended to be a consumer guide or a comprehensive history of the pub. The selection, ranging from the smallest traditional pub to the large Georgian inns of the coaching era, encompasses all periods of history from the alehouses of the Middle Ages to the galleried courtyard inns of the Elizabethan strolling players and the canal-side pubs of the Industrial Revolution. Travelling around the country it became apparent to me that modernization and expansion were spoiling the character of many rural buildings, and that contemporary commercial pressures were fast destroying one of our most unique and enduring institutions. I decided, therefore, to try and record some of these enchanting places before the twentieth century took over completely. Making my selection proved a near impossible task given the variety and diversity of pubs throughout the country, so I have tried to feature wherever possible those pubs with historical or literary associations, or whose setting, whether in the heart of the country or close to the sea, is a picture of rustic charm.

Inn, public house, alehouse and tavern are all names that have been applied to the pub over the years. Although the differences between them are now blurred, originally their

WARREN HOUSE
POSTBRIDGE, DEVON

Totally isolated, Warren House lies on the road across Dartmoor that leads to the famous prison. The pub was built in 1845 to cater for local Devon tin-miners. At one end of the bar is a peat-burning fire, that has supposedly been kept burning continuously since the pub opened.

functions were different and clearly defined. An hotel is the modern equivalent of the inn, which not only offered food on a more substantial scale than a pub, but also provided accommodation to travellers. The village pub is a descendant of the alehouse, smaller in scale than the inn, it did not provide accommodation legally until the seventeenth century. The tavern was the urban equivalent of the alehouse, but served mainly wine, not beer.

The derivation of pubs' names is a fascinating subject, and through some simple detective work they can reveal a slice of social history. Many names relate to a local occupation such as The Plough or The Shepherd and Dog, or a pastime, The Bat and Ball or The Fox and Hounds, or commemorate a local family. The names of inns with medieval origins are frequently connected with the Church or heraldry. During the Dissolution however, many names were secularized and quickly The Pope's Head became The King's Head; not surprisingly Henry VIII is the most commonly portrayed king on English pub signs. The Red Lion, Golden Lion, and The Unicorn are all names borrowed from heraldry, as is The White Hart, which was also the emblem of Richard II. The Feathers, a name derived from the emblem of successive Princes of Wales was another popular royal choice, like The Royal Oak which commemorates Charles II's famous hiding-place from the Parliamentarians.

The emergence of CAMRA (the Campaign for Real Ale) has renewed peoples' taste for beer brewed in the traditional way by small independent companies that are consequently enjoying a well-deserved prosperity. Exploring the countryside in search of secluded pubs where a pint of real ale can be enjoyed in a traditional atmosphere is now a popular pastime, helping to preserve the individuality and diversity so characteristic of the English country pub.

FOX AND HOUNDS
EXTON, LEICESTERSHIRE

Exton was originally in Rutland, England's smallest county, which was incorporated into Leicestershire in 1974. Although now a quiet backwater, it was once on the main coaching route to Oakham.

The area was renowned for its fox-hunting, a fact reflected in the name of this tall stone coaching inn whose walls are covered with hunting and military prints. The famous Cottesmore Hunt was formed in Exton in 1772 but has since been relocated. The Fox and Hounds overlooks the village green where hunts met regularly.

HISTORICAL PUBS AND INNS

CAT AND FIDDLE
HINTON ADMIRAL,
HAMPSHIRE

The walls of the Cat and Fiddle are of cob and the roof a very deep thatch. There was a hospice here as early as the eleventh century. Run by the monks of Christchurch Priory, it offered shelter and refuge to travellers in the New Forest, in those days a wild and dangerous place. It was known as the house of Caterine la Fidele (derived from the Latin for St Catherine the Faithful), and was recorded as such in the Domesday Book. It is likely that this is the derivation of the pub's present name even though the sign depicts the nursery rhyme.

During the eighteenth and nineteenth centuries the pub became the haunt of smugglers operating in Christchurch Bay; one of the chimneys having a secret hiding-place for contraband.

The majority of England's population in the early Middle Ages eked out a meagre living from the land, tied in serfdom after the Conquest to a new Norman aristocracy. There were few reasons or opportunities to travel any distance: trade had not yet become established, and the country, thickly forested and sparsely populated, was difficult to traverse. The Church, which held such influence over peoples' lives, provided the main motive for travel. A pilgrimage to one of the recognized shrines at, for example, Glastonbury, Canterbury or Chichester, offered the hope of obtaining spiritual salvation and even, supposedly, physical healing.

Under monastic rules of hospitality the monks were obliged to offer food and shelter to any traveller in need and so hospices were built near monasteries to accommodate the pilgrims. All travellers would share one room, eating from long wooden tables and sleeping on rush-strewn floors. Standards, however, gradually improved, and wealthier pilgrims were soon able to enjoy private rooms. Many of these hospices became so prosperous that despite their religious connections they survived the Dissolution of the early sixteenth century and continued to flourish after their associated monasteries had disappeared. Inns that originated as hospices are mainly found in southern England, where the more important shrines were located; The George and Pilgrim in Glastonbury and The George at Norton St Philip are two of the best surviving examples.

Another group of inns whose origins are connected with the Church are those built to provide accommodation for the teams of medieval church-builders who travelled round the country. These 'houses' often continued to offer hospitality to wayfarers and travellers after the local church was completed, frequently being run by the local priest to provide him with additional income. The south-west of England has a number of pubs still known as Church House, including the one at Rattery in Devon.

The medieval manor house was also a source of hospitality. Some lords built guest-houses to be run as inns by their stewards, while in other cases the manor house would be converted into an inn when the lord had a new, larger house built nearby. Many of these historic inns still bear the family name and arms.

PUNCHBOWL INN
LANREATH, CORNWALL

An interesting wrought-iron sign, said to have been designed by Augustus John, hangs outside the Punchbowl, whose functions over the years have included court house, coaching inn and centre for the distribution of smugglers' contraband.

When in use as a court house, two rooms were set aside for serving ale, mead and cider to witnesses and plaintiffs, one room for the lower classes, the other for the gentry. The rooms, which are used as bars today, are appropriately called the Men's Kitchen and the Farmers' Kitchen.

The inn has its own well, now covered since the introduction of mains water. It was known as St Monarch's well and was reputed to have miraculous properties.

CASTLE INN
LYDFORD, DEVON

The austere Norman keep of Lydford Castle dominates its Dartmoor village of granite houses and the pink-washed Castle Inn. When tin mining was a major industry the keep was used as both court and prison for offenders against the harsh stannary laws. A seventeenth-century ballad by local poet William Browne includes some chilling words:

I oft have heard of Lydford
   Law
How in the morning they hang
   and draw
And sit in judgement after.

Both bars of the Tudor inn have low, beamed ceilings, log fires and polished flagstone floors. The walls are colourfully decorated with early cigarette cards, Victorian posters and royal commemorative plates.

HARDWICK INN
HARDWICK HALL, DERBYSHIRE

The magnificent Elizabethan mansion was built in 1597 for the Dowager Countess of Shrewsbury, 'Bess of Hardwick'. Tall and symmetrical with a tower at each corner, the whole building seems to be full of windows. The Great Chamber is one of the finest in the country and has superb tapestries on display.

Hardwick Hall is in the care of the National Trust, which has also preserved the sixteenth-century Grand Lodge at the entrance to the grounds and turned it into a pub, the Hardwick Inn.

The inn is of the same golden stone as the Hall and many of the rooms still feel like those of a private country house, decorated with elegant wallpaper and lit by daylight filtering through mullioned lattice windows.

THE CHURCH HOUSE
RATTERY, DEVON

Rattery, on the southern fringes of Dartmoor, has one of the 'Church Houses' common to the region. Probably built both as a monks' hospice and to provide accommodation for the builders of the local church, it dates back to 1028 and has a fine spiral stone staircase almost as old as the building itself. The timbers used inside the inn are huge and roughly hewn, as one might expect from their age. Two old fireplaces have recently been uncovered and restored using local stone.

The first vicar of Rattery was appointed in 1199, the year King John came to the throne, and a complete list of all subsequent vicars is hung in one of the bars.

WHITE BULL
RIBCHESTER, LANCASHIRE

In the first century AD, Ribchester was an important Roman fort named Bremetennacum, situated on a curve of the River Ribble. The fort occupied some five acres and extensive remains have been uncovered. One particularly dramatic find from the site was a Roman ceremonial helmet that is now kept in the British Museum.

The seventeenth-century White Bull has a porch supported by four complete Tuscan columns that were originally part of the fort. A roughly carved white bull stands out from the wall above the porch and probably dates from the eighteenth century.

In the late eighteenth century the White Bull functioned as the local court house for many years, and one of its rooms was used as a holding cell. Evidence for this emerged when a set of leg irons was discovered firmly attached to one of the walls.

FLEUR-DE-LIS
STOKE SUB HAMDON, SOMERSET

As its name suggests, the village lies under the lee of Hamdon, or Ham Hill, and it is from here that the distinctive golden building stone is quarried. In common with most of the village buildings, the seventeenth-century Fleur-de-Lis has the lovely mellow, textured exterior associated with this outstanding limestone.

The inn is particularly notable for its original fives court at the rear of the building. Fives was a ball game usually played against church walls from the fourteenth century onwards, but it took such a hold in the West Country that many inns erected their own courts for the benefit of their customers.

THE CASTLE INN
EDGE HILL, WARWICKSHIRE

It was on beech-clad Edge Hill that Charles I raised his standard in 1642 before the first major battle of the Civil War. The octagonal castellated folly that now forms part of The Castle Inn was built in 1749 by Sanderson Miller, a local squire, to commemorate the battle.

The walls of the main bar are decorated with weapons including swords and pistols, and with photographs taken during filmed re-enactments of the battle.

It is said that at certain times the sound of fighting can still be heard and that a ghostly cavalry officer gallops through the bar.

KING'S ARMS
OMBERSLEY, HEREFORD AND WORCESTER

Ombersley boasts an outstanding collection of the black-and-white half-timbered houses typical of the region, more than twenty being listed buildings. One of the most notable is the King's Arms, which dates back to 1411. It still retains in one of its bars a superbly decorated seventeenth-century plaster ceiling. King Charles was said to have taken shelter here while fleeing from the Roundheads.

On the village green is a rare example of a 'plague stone', a relic from the Black Death of 1348. Villagers would put money in the stone trough so that traders could leave their goods and collect payment, thereby avoiding the risk of infection.

THE GEORGE AND PILGRIM
GLASTONBURY, SOMERSET

Glastonbury is steeped in legend and this ancient pilgrims' hostel preserves the atmosphere of centuries past. Built in 1475 by Abbot John de Selwood, it accommodated the wealthier pilgrims who came to visit Glastonbury Abbey, which supposedly occupied the same site as a chapel built by Joseph of Arimathea in AD 63. After the dissolution of the monasteries in the sixteenth century the pilgrims' hostel was converted into an inn, but it retained many of its ecclesiastical features and much of its original character is still preserved today.

One of the George's bedrooms is named after Henry VIII who, it is said, watched from its window while the Abbey burned.

Glastonbury is also the centre of the Arthurian legends and is regarded by many as being Avalon, King Arthur's final resting place.

SMITH'S ARMS
GODMANSTONE, DORSET

England's smallest inn was granted a licence by King Charles II. The story alleges that the king stopped in Godmanstone to have his horse shod at the blacksmith's shop, asked for a drink and, when refused, granted the smith a licence on the spot.

The tiny one-roomed pub is built of flint and has a deep thatched roof. A colourful sign rests over the timber porch, which leads to an interior decorated with National Hunt racing pictures.

Just a few miles up the road is the dramatic Cerne Abbas hill figure. Fifteen hundred years old and 180 feet high, it depicts a naked man holding a club and may be associated with ancient fertility rites.

THE CASTLE INN
CHIDDINGSTONE, KENT

So unspoiled are the sixteenth- and seventeenth-century houses here that they have been used as period film locations. The National Trust administers the village and The Castle Inn, which is at the end of a row of houses that faces the long churchyard. Almost completely hung with red tiles, The Castle has been an inn since 1730, when it was called the Five Bells.

Behind the village school stands a huge sandstone block that is called the 'Chiding Stone'. Legend states that it was where women were brought to be reprimanded for gossiping or causing a nuisance. Although an intriguing theory, it is not thought to be how the village acquired its name.

The castle after which the inn is now named is actually a seventeenth-century mansion that was given a Gothic exterior in the nineteenth century complete with towers and turrets.

OLD SWAN
MINSTER LOVELL, OXFORDSHIRE

The delightfully named Cotswold river, the Windrush, flows gently around Minster Lovell with its ruined hall, fifteenth-century bridge and ancient inn.

Huge open log fires, flagstone floors covered with Turkish rugs and low, beamed ceilings add to the atmosphere of the fourteenth-century Old Swan. Guests over the years have ranged from Welsh sheep drovers to retainers of King Richard III. The king's emblem, the 'Sun in Splendour' has been found beneath plasterwork in one of the bedrooms, although Richard himself probably stayed at Minster Lovell Hall with his loyal friend, Francis Lovell.

Poor Francis Lovell suffered a bizarre and lonely death at the Hall. Having been declared a traitor by Henry VII he went into hiding, but the only servant who knew his whereabouts died suddenly leaving his master to starve. His skeleton was found some two hundred years later, still seated at a table.

THE WEARY FRIAR
PILLATON, CORNWALL

The whitewashed L-shaped inn is overshadowed by the granite bulk of St Odulph's, Pillaton's twelfth-century church. The masons who built it were accommodated in what is now The Weary Friar but would then have been several cottages. They have been converted over the years to form the comfortable inn that exists today.

It is thought that at one time the inn may also have been a rest house for a Dominican friary and it is this connection that has provided the present name. Until 1963 it was called the Royal Oak.

THE GEORGE
CASTLE CARY, SOMERSET

The George is an ancient thatched inn dating back to 1452 and built of stones from the nearby Norman castle of which only the foundations remain. An inglenook fireplace in one of the bars is original and its supporting elm was growing as a young tree in AD 900.

Charles II stayed here while fleeing from Cromwell after the battle of Worcester in 1651. Across the road, behind the market hall, is a curious beehive structure. This was the village lock-up, built in 1779 it has gratings instead of windows and cost the princely sum of £23 to build.

THE KING'S ARMS INN
MONTACUTE, SOMERSET

St Michael's Hill rises sharply behind Montacute, which is one of the most attractive villages in Somerset, being built in mellow, golden Ham Hill stone. The village derives its name from the Latin *mons acutus*, meaning steep hill. In the ninth century, however, Montacute was known as Bishopston, now the name of the street that runs north from the church of St Catherine.

Next to the church is the creeper-clad King's Arms, an elegant early Georgian building. The pub has been modernized sensitively and the atmosphere of the eighteenth century still lingers inside.

Montacute House is regarded as one of the finest Elizabethan mansions in the country and has a gallery 189 feet long, running the entire length of the second floor. It was built for Sir Edward Phelips, Speaker of the House of Commons, who opened the case for the prosecution against Guy Fawkes in 1606.

THE SPEECH HOUSE
FOREST OF DEAN, GLOUCESTERSHIRE

Formerly a royal hunting forest, the fifty square miles of the Forest of Dean is perhaps the most impressive area of unbroken woodland left in England today. At its very heart is the Speech House, a three-storey sandstone building completed in the 1670s and home of the Verderer's Court, which was set up to settle disputes between iron founders and foresters in addition to trying people for such offences as poaching royal venison. At one time the court had the power to condemn a man to death. The court still functions today in the inn's dining-room, sitting every three months and dealing with matters connected with the Forest by-laws.

Prior to the seventeenth century the ancient Speech Court, thought to be the oldest court of law in England, was held in a building called Kenesley, which occupied the same site as the present inn.

ROSE AND CROWN
BAINBRIDGE, NORTH YORKSHIRE

The fifteenth-century Rose and Crown lies at one end of the large village green around which the houses and cottages of Bainbridge cluster.

Bainbridge and the Rose and Crown still continue an ancient tradition that has survived for over seven hundred years: forest horn blowing. Every night from Holy Rood Day in September to Shrovetide in spring, a great buffalo horn is carried outside the pub and three long sonorous notes reverberate around the hills of Wensleydale. The task has been undertaken by the same family for generations.

This custom probably originated to guide shepherds, drovers and travellers down from the desolate fells at dusk. The present horn hangs next to a much older one, said to date from the fourteenth century.

THE BAT AND BALL
HAMBLEDON, HAMPSHIRE

The sharp crack of leather on willow echoes across Broadhalfpenny Down as it has for over two hundred years. This was an early home of English cricket and the Hambledon Club of the 1770s was responsible for introducing some of the rules that govern the game today. When the club was playing, the inn served as pavilion and clubhouse. The team's moment of glory came in 1777 when it defeated an All England XI by an innings and sixty-eight runs.

John Nyrens wrote the first cricketing manual in 1833 and in it appeared advertisements for the beer at the Bat and Ball. The ale cost twopence a pint and 'would put the soul of three butchers into one weaver'.

STAR AND EAGLE
GOUDHURST, KENT

At the highest point of the village, the Star and Eagle commands fine views over the hop fields and orchards of the Weald. The building was once a monastery and traces of fourteenth-century stone vaulting are still visible. A secret tunnel once ran from the inn's cellar to the neighbouring church.

Towards the end of the eighteenth century the inn was the headquarters of a notorious gang of smugglers who terrorized the district. The villagers eventually fought a pitched battle with the villains and routed them and the gang's leader was caught and later hanged from a gibbet on nearby Horsemonden Heath.

YE OLDE BELL
HURLEY, BERKSHIRE

Ye Olde Bell was once the guest-house of Hurley Priory, an eleventh-century Benedictine monastery. The inn itself dates back to 1135 and although largely rebuilt in the sixteenth century, features such as the stone entrance survive from the original. A hidden tunnel led from the Olde Bell to the priory building but is no longer accessible.

Behind the inn is a magnificent garden where the monks once cut reeds for the priory floor. It is but a short walk down to the river Thames, where a regatta is now held in mid-August.

YE OLDE FIGHTING COCKS

ST ALBANS,
HERTFORDSHIRE

Occupying part of the site of a monastery founded by King Offa in AD 793, the Fighting Cocks claims to be one of the oldest inns in England. It is a small eleventh-century octagonal timber-framed dove-cote, that was re-erected here in 1599 when it became an inn.

During the seventeenth and eighteenth centuries it was the local cock-fighting centre until the sport was banned in 1849. It was renamed The Fisherman but has since reverted to its original title.

The inn has recently been modernized, the sunken cockpit being successfully incorporated into the bar area.

THE STAR INN

ALFRISTON, EAST SUSSEX

Once known as the Star of Bethlehem, this medieval inn was run by the monks of Battle Abbey as a hospice for pilgrims travelling to the shrine of St Richard at Chichester.

The timber-framed frontage is covered with remarkable carvings. The Star's best known feature, however, is the grotesque red lion that stands at one corner and which is thought to have been the figurehead from a Dutch warship sunk by the Duke of York in 1672 at the battle of Sole Bay.

Inside the inn is a wooden pillar that was once a sanctuary post giving fugitives from the law instant Church protection and freedom from prosecution.

THE BEAR INN
BISLEY,
GLOUCESTERSHIRE

Bisley is an isolated village on the south-west fringes of the Cotswolds. Because of its position it has been nicknamed Bisley-God-Help-Us, a reference to the harsh winter winds that sweep across the hillside.

Steep narrow streets wind through the village of greystone houses and cottages. At the top of George Street is The Bear Inn. Parts of The Bear date from the sixteenth century, although the four fine columns that support the upper floor are seventeenth century. In common with other country inns, The Bear was once used as a court house and the old village lock-up, dated 1824, is nearby.

THE OLD MINT
SOUTHAM,
WARWICKSHIRE

Originally a monks' hospice, this pub's medieval heritage is evident from the irregular stonework of the building and the mullioned windows. A mint was established here in the seventeenth century when it was apparently used by Charles I during the Civil War to melt down silver for coin to pay his army before the battle of Edge Hill. It also produced Southam 'tokens', a special local currency of low denomination, the coin of the realm being too highly valued for everyday use.

Inside The Old Mint the half-timbered walls of the bars display an impressive array of weaponry, ranging from guns and powder flasks to pikes and cutlasses. Behind the bar is a slightly more peaceful collection of toby jugs.

WHITE HART
FYFIELD, OXFORDSHIRE

Sir John Golafre, Lord of the Manor of Fyfield, died in 1442 and left money to build and endow a chantry house and hospital for the poor, to be run by a priest. When chantries were abolished in the sixteenth century the building was bought by St John's College, Oxford, which subsequently leased it as an inn.

Renovation took place in 1963 and the hall has been restored to its original state, revealing the impressive fifteenth-century gallery. The priest's room and barrel-vaulted cellar have been converted into restaurants. One of the side bars contains a very old inglenook fireplace, complete with enormous black urn suspended over the grate.

THE GEORGE INN
NORTON ST PHILIP, SOMERSET

The George Inn was built by the Carthusian monks of Hinton Charterhouse in 1397 as a guest-house for visiting wool merchants. The monks were sheep farmers and the village held important wool fairs during the fourteenth and fifteenth centuries.

The Duke of Monmouth made the inn his headquarters in 1685 prior to the battle of Sedgemoor, a bloody encounter that ended his rebellion against James II.

A small galleried courtyard gives a good indication of what the inn was like originally. One floor of the building was used as a store and the steps up to the waggon-loading platform still remain. The bars are simply furnished with antique settles and tables and the high, beamed ceilings are hung with harnesses and copper pans. This is one of the best surviving medieval inns in England.

COACHING INNS

The history of coaching inns is inseparable from that of the development of the English road network. Although we may often complain about the state of our roads, they are a far cry from the rutted tracks, maintained by parish labour, that served as highways until the mid-seventeenth century. By the end of the Civil War a limited stage-coach service had been established on the major highways leading out of London to Winchester, York and Newcastle, but it was not until the introduction of the first Turnpike Act in 1663 that any progress was made towards establishing a better system of roads. This Act empowered business trusts, usually supported by local interest, to construct roads and recoup the cost by levying tolls, any additional income earned would then be invested in new building and repairs.

The early, hesitant days of this new form of transport provided travellers with something of an endurance test. Appalling road conditions combined with unsprung coaches made travelling any distance a physical nightmare. John Cresset, writing in 1672, had the following to say about coach travel: 'What advantage is it to Man's health, to be called out of their Beds into these Coaches an hour before day in the morning, to be hurried in them from place to place, till one hour, two, or three within night. . . . often brought into their Inns by Torchlight, when it is too late to sit up and get a Supper.'

Although there had been a sprinkling of taverns and alehouses along the highways as early as the fourteenth century, roadside inns did not begin to flourish until the mid-seventeenth century when the coaching network became more fully established. By the 1750s huge improvements in road conditions and carriage design had been made. The stamina of coach horses, however, limited the distances that could be covered to between twelve and fifteen miles each stage. The increased volume of road traffic resulted in the building of many new inns and the conversion and expansion of older inns to include stable blocks and better accommodation.

In 1784, John Palmer of Bath introduced his revolutionary plan of carrying mail by coach, and by the late eighteenth century there were over 20,000 miles of turnpike roads and mail coaches had become the major form of public transport. Posting houses sprang up along the major routes to provide refreshment for travellers, change of horses and postilions. The innkeeper would act as local postmaster, either delivering the mail himself or keeping it until collected; The George and Dragon at Hurstbourne Tarrant still has its old pigeon-holed letter box. The golden age of coaching was in full swing.

By the end of the eighteenth century the larger inns were offering a high degree of service and comfort. Even if a coach was only scheduled to stop for half an hour to change horses and allow the passengers to dine, waiters would be standing in readiness at the inn's doorway to take cloaks, shawls and hats and the landlord and landlady would be in the hall to welcome their guests. A large table with a selection of cold meats, game pies and cheeses would be the choice set before the traveller. Passengers who stayed overnight usually disembarked in the courtyard and could spend a comfortable night in a well-furnished bedroom with four-poster bed, fireplace and private parlour.

The coaching era in its heyday was perhaps the high point in the history of the inn. Most of England's market towns possess at least one Georgian inn and many others have older buildings that were modernized during this period to keep pace with their rivals. The black-and-white half-timbered inns that we now consider so charming were thought to be old-fashioned and ugly in the eighteenth century, and many of them were covered in a layer of brick or plaster to present a more fashionable and up-to-date façade. Fortunately, some of the best examples of timber-frame inns have had their false exteriors removed and have been restored to their original condition, the Georgian plaster covering fortuitously acting as a timber preservative in many cases; The Feathers at Ledbury being a superb example. The Georgian inn became the focal point of local society and many of the larger inns possessed assembly rooms and palatial ballrooms. These large inns have, in many cases, now become hotels, but evidence of their colourful heritage can be seen in the fine elaborate high ceilings and ornate fireplaces. Towards the 1830s some inns became even more extravagant and huge porticos were added to the façades to indicate their great importance.

This period proved to be the coaching inn's finest but final hour, the railways had arrived and in a very short space of time most long-distance road travel had disappeared. Many inns went out of business; some survived running coach services to the local railway stations and others remained dormant until the motor car took people and goods onto the roads again and gave the roadside inns a new lease of life.

KIRKSTONE PASS INN
AMBLESIDE, CUMBRIA

Formerly known as the Traveller's Rest, the inn is one of the highest in England. On a typical Lake District day when the wind drives the rain horizontally across the fells, it does not require much imagination to conjure up images of steaming, straining horses hauling the Penrith coach up the steep ascent on an unmade road.

Although considerably altered over the years to cope with motorized trade it still has a good deal of atmosphere, especially during the winter months when the fires really get blazing. The building itself dates back to the seventeenth century but the pub was not licensed until the nineteenth.

WHITE HART INN
SOMERTON, SOMERSET

In the days of the West Saxons, Somerset was part of the kingdom of Wessex, which also included Dorset and Wiltshire. It was from Wessex that King Alfred the Great led the fight against the Danes in the ninth century. Somerton, with its Anglo-Saxon castle, was an important stronghold. A coaching inn during the eighteenth century on the route from Bristol to Weymouth, the White Hart was originally built on the site of the castle and some of the masonry has been incorporated into the inn.

The White Hart stands on one edge of the market square which has an old cross, rebuilt in 1673.

THE FEATHERS
LUDLOW, SHROPSHIRE

The elaborately carved timber-framed façade of The Feathers is impressive. Dating back to 1603, it was meticulously restored in 1970. The interior of the inn contains many original features including panelled rooms, moulded ceilings and royal coats of arms. Its name probably derives from the insignia of the Prince of Wales, Charles I having visited the inn in 1616 while he held that title.

Strategically sited, Ludlow was the seat of the Council of the Marches, which ruled the Welsh border country until disbanded by William III in 1689. The town's prosperity then declined and The Feathers was forced to close, but it reopened in 1752 as a coaching house with extensive stabling and has thrived ever since.

ANGEL AND WHITE HORSE
TADCASTER, NORTH YORKSHIRE

Tadcaster has long been a major brewing centre and the town today is dominated by the rival companies of Samuel and John Smith, the former being responsible for renovating and reopening the Angel as recently as 1976.

In the eighteenth century the town, some ten miles from York, was a busy coaching centre, and up to fifty public coaches a day passed through in addition to extensive private and goods trade. The fortunes of the inns and breweries have fluctuated over the years but Samuel Smith is now firmly established as one of the leading independent breweries producing real ale.

The inn's coachyard now provides stabling for the teams of shire horses that pull the brewery's dray waggons.

THE HAYCOCK
WANSFORD, CAMBRIDGESHIRE

For centuries Wansford has been the point where the Great North Road crosses the River Nene. The Haycock, which stands close to the bridge, was built in 1632 on the site of a previous inn.

The Haycock was quite an important posting station with stabling for 150 horses in the yard and it was here, in 1870, that the legendary jockey Fred Archer began his career.

Towards the end of the nineteenth century business declined to such an extent that The Haycock closed and became a farm for a time. It was later used as a racing stable by Lionel Digby who kept 100 horses in training and the building finally reverted to its original function in 1928.

DUN COW
DUNCHURCH, WARWICKSHIRE

In common with many other inns, the Dun Cow was largely rebuilt in the late eighteenth century to cope with the coaching trade, however, many older parts are still in evidence. It was supposed to have been one of the haunts of Dick Turpin, England's most famous highwayman.

Slightly more respectable visitors included George Stephenson, the early rail pioneer, who is remembered for his engine, 'The Rocket'. He dined here with his son Robert to celebrate the opening of a tunnel on the Birmingham to London railway, which they had just completed.

THE FEATHERS
LEDBURY, HEREFORD AND WORCESTER

Ledbury was the birthplace of Poet Laureate John Masefield and is still more or less as he described it: 'pleasant to the sight, fair and half timbered houses black and white'. None more so than The Feathers. Built in 1565, its entire frontage is a jumbled mass of narrowly spaced beams and windows. The third storey with five gables was added in the seventeenth century.

As the coaching trade increased, a Georgian wing was added at the rear of the inn and the timbers on the front plastered over to make the building seem 'less old fashioned'. Fortunately the owners did not pull it down and rebuild as many did during that period and the plaster was eventually removed in the nineteenth century.

THE GEORGE AND DRAGON
HURSTBOURNE TARRANT, HAMPSHIRE

The George and Dragon, part of which dates from the sixteenth century, is the sole survivor of five inns that once competed for the coaching trade in Hurstbourne Tarrant. Formerly known as Uphusband, the village is just to the north of Hurstbourne Hill, one of the steepest and straightest hills in England.

Teams of horses were frequently changed here so that fresh animals could tackle the severe gradient. A local farmer, Joseph Blount, often lent his cart-horse to assist the heavier goods waggons and, having reached the summit, the horse would come back alone finding his own way back to his stable.

The original oak mail rack where letters delivered by coach awaited collection is still in the bar.

THE GEORGE
HUNTINGDON, CAMBRIDGESHIRE

A strategic site sixty miles from London on the Great North Road ensured that The George has always been well patronized. Even before its heyday in the coaching era it was a well-known stop-over on the journey north to York and beyond.

A fire in 1870 destroyed much of the main building but fortunately the two seventeenth-century wings survived. One of these is a rare example of an original open gallery overlooking the yard and is now used for the performance of Shakespearian plays.

Oliver Cromwell was born and raised in Huntingdon and records show that in 1574 his grandfather, Henry Cromwell, was The George's owner.

THE KING'S ARMS
AMERSHAM, BUCKINGHAMSHIRE

Despite being in the front line of Buckinghamshire's commuter belt, Amersham still retains the character of an ancient market town. First granted a charter by King John in 1200, it later became an important staging post on the London to Aylesbury run.

The jettied gables of the sixteenth-century King's Arms overlook the broad High Street, which contains several other old coaching inns. A mellow atmosphere prevails inside with its original alcoves, beams and oak flooring. Through the arched coach entrance is a small flower-filled courtyard.

A short distance away stands the seventeenth-century market hall, built on pillars with the town's old lock-up at its centre.

THE KING'S ARMS
TREGONY, CORNWALL

Tregony is a stone-built village with wide streets close to the River Fal, a few miles inland from the 'Cornish Riviera'. In the coaching era it was on a route via the county's cathedral city, Truro, to Falmouth. Sir Walter Raleigh was one of the first people to recognize the importance of Falmouth's location and the potential of its fine natural harbour, and the town sprang to prominence in the early seventeenth century.

The King's Arms dates from 1615 and has a rather grand-looking pillared entrance porch, and inside some fine Jacobean panelling. The arched entrance to the coach-yard still exists. King Charles I is reputed to have stayed at the inn, probably on a visit to his supporters; nearby Pendennis Castle, which looks down over Falmouth, was the last Royalist stronghold to fall to Cromwell.

THE LION
BUCKDEN, CAMBRIDGESHIRE

Buckden High Street was once part of the Great North Road, improved by Edward I in the thirteenth century when marching his armies north to repel the Scots. The inn stands next to the impressive ruins of Buckden Palace, home of the bishops of Lincoln from medieval times until 1838.

Originally a guest-house to the Palace, The Lion was considerably extended in the eighteenth century to meet the needs of coach-borne travellers. At the same time another inn was built across the road and they shared the traffic; one taking the London-bound trade, the other the north-bound.

Traces of the inn's religious past can be seen on a carved boss where the ceiling timbers meet in what was once the great hall. The carving is of a lamb and carries the inscription, '*Ecce Agnus Dei*' (Behold the Lamb of God).

THE BELL
STILTON, CAMBRIDGESHIRE

Once an important staging post on the Great North Road, Stilton's wide main street has a more tranquil air now that the village has been bypassed by the main road. The Bell is an elegant building of mellow Northamptonshire stone built in 1515, and altered in 1642. Its sign is suspended far out over the pavement by an elaborate network of wrought-iron supports.

Stilton cheese is famous world-wide, but it is doubtful whether it was ever made here; Melton Mowbray in Leicestershire has been producing the cheese since at least 1730. The cheese, however, was sold to coach passengers who broke their journey at Stilton, and it was also shipped down to London from here and gradually assumed the name of the village.

THE BULL
BRIDPORT, DORSET

Bridport, the 'Port Bredy' of Thomas Hardy's novels, was once a noted rope-making centre. The town's wide pavements were known as 'ropewalks' because the new ropes were laid out along them for twisting and drying.

The Bull, which dates from the sixteenth century, was an important stopping-place on the route from London to the West Country. Like the crack trains of the steam era, the coaches often had exciting and evocative names, such as the 'Royal Mail', the 'Eclipse', the 'Celerity' and the 'Regulator'. The arrival of the railways sounded the death knell for many coaching inns, but The Bull showed a degree of enterprise by running its own coach from Bridport station to the popular seaside resort of Lyme Regis.

THE SWAN
FITTLEWORTH, WEST SUSSEX

Parts of The Swan date from the fifteenth century and earlier. The upper storey is tile-hung and some of the original Horsham slates are still on the roof. It became a posting house in the eighteenth century and the hay racks from the stables are now used as flower baskets to adorn the front of the inn.

Landscape artist John Constable lodged here when on painting expeditions. This area, just to the north of the South Downs, has always attracted artists, examples of whose work may usually be seen in the hotel.

Hanging in the hall is one of the hotel's old inn signs, dating from 1900 and depicting a woman astride a swan. The figure was originally nude until it was noticed how similar her face was to Queen Victoria's, whereupon she hastily received a decent covering.

WHITE LION
WHERWELL, HAMPSHIRE

The White Lion is a tastefully renovated coaching inn whose thatched stables have been converted into additional bars. The inn stands on the hill that drops down into Wherwell, a village where one can truly appreciate the craft of the thatcher. So many shapes and styles of thatch grace the houses and cottages that it appears to have become an art form rather than a mere roof covering.

Fragments remain of Wherwell Abbey, founded by Queen Elfrida in AD 986. The mother of King Ethelred the Unready, she built the Abbey as a penance for the murder of her stepson, King Edward.

HOOPS INN
HORNS CROSS, DEVON

Midway between Bideford and Clovelly and just a mile from the sea, this long, beautifully thatched inn has been serving travellers since the thirteenth century, eventually becoming a notable coaching inn on the main north coast route to Cornwall. It was particularly famous for its home-brewed ale, the water for which came from an ancient well in the bar-room floor.

Before the coaching trade developed, the Hoops Inn was a notorious smugglers' haunt. One of the West Country's greatest villains, a pirate and murderer called Coppinger, lived in the district for ten years and was probably a regular at the Hoops.

HARDWICKE ARMS
ARRINGTON, CAMBRIDGESHIRE

Built in the thirteenth century for travellers on Ermine Street, one of the main Roman roads running from London to the Humber, the inn now incorporates six different periods of architecture.

It probably acquired its present name in the eighteenth century from the owners of nearby Wimpole Hall. Philip Yorke, Baron Hardwicke, who bought the Hall in 1740 became 1st Earl of Hardwicke in 1754. The family lived in the Hall for generations until the entire estate was lost in a wager. Both the Hall and Wimpole Home Farm are now owned by the National Trust.

Early in the nineteenth century the Hardwicke Arms was used by the Land Commission as a conference centre when allocating estates to victorious generals returning from the Napoleonic Wars.

DEVONSHIRE ARMS
BEELEY, DERBYSHIRE

Beeley is a village of narrow twisting lanes at the southern end of the Chatsworth estate, a park that contains one of the greatest stately homes in England. The house was built for the 1st Duke of Devonshire in 1707 and is world-famous for its art collections.

The Devonshire Arms originated as three cottages in 1726, and these were converted into an inn in 1741. During the late eighteenth century it was a prosperous coaching inn serving the route between Bakewell and Matlock. It has exposed stone walls, black beams and huge fireplaces, one of which contains a small pool and waterfall. Coins thrown into it are given to charity.

TRADITIONAL PUBS AND INNS

For many people the typical English pub, like its frequent village neighbours the church and the manor house, is evocative of an idyllic country life. The fifteenth-century Royal Oak at Cardington presents such an image; nestling in a valley and standing almost in the shadow of the village church, the white-washed and timber-frame building is in complete harmony with its surroundings.

Built from local materials in a regional architectural style, the country inn displays a wealth of history and tradition. It is intimately linked to the community it serves, like the lonely Tan Hill Inn in North Yorkshire, which originated in the eighteenth century to cater for the coal miners who worked in this remote area, or Fulking's Shepherd and Dog, conveniently sited on the droving route across the South Downs to Findon sheep market. For centuries the traditional pub has provided a convivial atmosphere where news and gossip can be exchanged, its clientele usually made up of regulars and occasional visitors – unlike the larger coaching inns that thrived on a more impersonal and transitory trade.

What we now think of as the traditional pub would probably have originated as the village alehouse, fulfilling much the same role as its modern counterpart. The humblest of these alehouses would simply have been the kitchen of a labourer's cottage, his wife perhaps brewing enough ale for the whole village, with any surplus being offered to travellers; thus the trade developed. The alehouse distinguished itself from its neighbouring buildings by a bunch of green leaves or branches tied to the end of a pole suspended above the door. A similar system had been used by the Romans who tied vine leaves outside their taverns. This simple but effective means of identification was the precursor of the painted inn sign and many pubs around the country still incorporate the word 'bush' into their names, a reminder of this ancient symbol.

In the Middle Ages ale was virtually the only drink available apart from water, which was often dangerous because of the crude drainage and unhealthy sanitation. Tea was not introduced into the country until the seventeenth century. Medieval ale was quite weak, being low in alcohol and brewed without hops. Hops were brought into the

GEORGE AND DRAGON
GARRIGIL, CUMBRIA

A cottage pub of great character, the beer is still served from the cellar of the George and Dragon in the traditional manner, straight from the cask. During the summer the village green may be littered with bodies in a state of near exhaustion, as Garrigill is the first point of civilization reached by walkers of the Pennine Way after climbing Cross Fell, the highest part of the walk.

country by Flemish weavers who settled in the south-east during the fourteenth century. Initially there was much opposition to the new 'hopped ale', which was considerably more bitter than the drink to which the English palate had become accustomed. It was called in Old English, *beor* – this being the derivation of our word 'beer' – and was the prototype of the many modern varieties of beer enjoyed today.

As trade in England developed and more and more people took to the roads, alehouses gradually expanded to provide refreshment for the increased number of travellers. Some established a good reputation for the quality of their brew, demand for which grew and led to the setting up of small-scale breweries serving customers within the range of a horse and cart. Even now there are a few areas, especially in the north of England, where beer is delivered by this traditional method, and the immaculately groomed shire horses pulling their drays can often be seen at county shows during the summer months.

Since CAMRA (the Campaign for Real Ale) waged war on the large brewing combines in the 1970s there has been a revival in the fortunes of the village pub and the small independent breweries that serve them. As the taste of traditionally brewed beer is becoming more popular so also is the idea of preserving the distinctive character of the country inn. Comfortable Windsor chairs in front of a blazing open fire form an agreeable picture for most of us, and the traditional games such as dominoes, darts, skittles and shove-halfpenny that would once have been a common sight are enjoying a revival too. Sadly, their incongruous modern electronic equivalents remain distressingly ubiquitous.

VICTORIA
EASTLEACH, GLOUCESTERSHIRE

The Victoria is an unpretentious and comfortable pub built at the turn of the century with a pleasant garden overlooking the rolling Cotswold landscape.

The village consists of two hamlets, Eastleach Turville and Eastleach Martin, separated by the River Leach, which is crossed by an ancient bridge built of huge flat paving-stones supported on stone piers. Despite their diminutive size each hamlet has its own church since they once belonged to different Norman landowners.

THE WENSLEYDALE HEIFER
WEST WITTON, NORTH YORKSHIRE

West Witton was a mining village when the Yorkshire Dales were an important centre for lead production. By the mid-nineteenth century, however, lead mining in the area had come to an end. The Wensleydale Heifer is a whitewashed stone inn that dates from the seventeenth century. It was a favourite haunt of James Herriot during his early days working as a vet in the Dales.

A centuries-old tradition is still observed in the village each year towards the end of August, the 'Burning of Bartle'. Bartle was apparently a local villain who stole livestock from the monks of Jervaulx Abbey. He was eventually caught and burned at the stake, an event that is celebrated by parading an effigy around the village before burning it at a place called Grass Gill End.

HOLLY BUSH INN
PRIORS MARSTON, WARWICKSHIRE

The Holly Bush is a fifteenth-century pub in what Sir Nikolaus Pevsner has described in his *Buildings of England* series as 'one of the most rewarding villages in this part of the country'. The pub and the attractive collection of houses and cottages that surround it are all built from the same golden coloured stone.

This rural area to the east of Leamington Spa is perfect riding country and the landlord has thoughtfully provided hitching-posts on the lawn for any customers who may arrive on horseback.

Inside the Holly Bush are a variety of rambling rooms with traditional pub furnishings and a copper-topped bar. A 'yard of ale' contest, a competition to see who can drink ale from a yard-high slender glass fastest, is still held every April Fool's Day.

OLDE ANCHOR INN
UPTON-ON-SEVERN, HEREFORD AND WORCESTER

Situated on the banks of the Severn, the charming market town of Upton is overlooked by the fourteenth-century tower of a now-demolished church. Topped with an eighteenth-century octagonal cupola, the tower together with the river setting gives the town a continental feel.

The Anchor is a sixteenth-century timber-framed building furnished inside with Windsor chairs, oak tables, old settles and lots of copper and brass, including an unusual copper mantlepiece.

At the rear of the pub is a small brewery and the Anchor offers its own beer together with other real ales.

THE CRISPIN INN
ASHOVER, DERBYSHIRE

Ashover is prettily situated beneath the hills on the edge of the Peak District. The Crispin Inn is said to date from 1416 and celebrates the return of Thomas Babington and others from the Battle of Agincourt, fought on St Crispin's Day.

A plaque on the pub's façade recounts a tale from 1646 when the landlord, Job Wall, tried to prevent some of King Charles I's troops from entering the inn as they were already drunk. They threw him out and set about drinking the pub completely dry, or so the story goes.

SHIPWRIGHT'S ARMS
HELFORD, CORNWALL

The village of Helford is at the end of one of the many steep winding lanes that lead down to the wooded creeks of the Helford river. Aptly named the 'Cornish Riviera', this area is renowned for its mild climate and sub-tropical vegetation.

The Shipwright's Arms is one of a cluster of thatched, whitewashed cob buildings that overlook the river. It was built in the eighteenth century when Helford was a small port that exported local tin to London. Now leisure boats and yachts frequent the peaceful inlet and the nautical atmosphere is reflected in the pub's interior where ships' lamps and old maritime paintings adorn the walls.

Across the river at Porth Navas are the oyster beds owned by the Duchy of Cornwall.

ALTISIDORA
BISHOP BURTON, HUMBERSIDE

The 400-year-old pub in Bishop Burton has been named after a succession of racehorses, Altisidora being the winner of England's oldest classic race, the St Leger, in 1813. The horse was owned by a Mr Watt whose house and grounds near the village are now an agricultural college.

The Altisidora is just across the road from the village duck pond, in the middle of which is an elegant war memorial. One corner of the village green is remembered as the place where the eighteenth-century evangelist John Wesley preached, and a bust carved from the elm under which he stood can be found in the parish church. He created such an impression that an open-air service is still held each year to commemorate his visit.

FARMERS' ARMS

BIRTSMORTON, HEREFORD AND WORCESTER

The Farmers' Arms is close to Birtsmorton Court, a picturesque moated house, parts of which date from the fourteenth century. The pub is some two centuries older; a black-and-white half-timbered house, typical of many in this region.

Unlike many pubs today, even those off the beaten track, this one has no jukebox or electronic space games to disturb the pleasant buzz of conversation and laughter. Outdoor skittles is one of the traditional games still enjoyed here.

SHEPHERD AND DOG

FULKING, WEST SUSSEX

The South Downs Way runs along the escarpment that overshadows the village of Fulking in the heart of Sussex sheep country. The path was used for centuries by shepherds and drovers driving their flocks across the Downs to market at Findon.

Built on a steep hill, at the bottom of which is a perpetual spring, the Shepherd and Dog was a stopping-place where the sheep and their guardians could both find refreshment. The pub is made up of two sixteenth-century cottages whose owners offered food and refreshment to the shepherds before the buildings were amalgamated and the pub licensed in 1735.

ROYAL OAK
CARDINGTON, SHROPSHIRE

The tiny Shropshire village of Cardington is sheltered by three surrounding hills and is dominated by its church. Immediately below the huge church tower is the fifteenth-century Royal Oak, whitewashed and timber-framed, a typical country pub whose furnishings and atmosphere are in keeping with its surroundings. High-backed settles and comfortable settees fill the many alcoves that radiate from the bar, which has a huge inglenook fireplace complete with black cauldron and hung about with many pewter jugs.

Near the village is Plaish Hall, the earliest brick-built house of its size in Shropshire and once the home of Judge William Leighton, chief Justice of Wales, who died in 1607.

RED LION
LLANFAIR WATERDINE, SHROPSHIRE

The Red Lion, which possibly dates back to the fourteenth century, overlooks the River Teme on the Welsh border. A path close to the pub leads to one of the best remaining stretches of Offa's Dyke, the defensive earthwork made by King Offa, the eighth-century King of Mercia. It runs from the River Dee in North Wales to the Wye in the south.

Llanfair Waterdine is not on the road to anywhere and its timeless atmosphere is reflected in the Red Lion. The taproom has an old polished red brick floor and a wood-burning stove in the great old fireplace.

COTTAGE OF CONTENT
CAREY, HEREFORD AND WORCESTER

Carey's rustic, medieval pub is aptly named. Located in a peaceful and unspoilt corner of England, it has been offering hospitality for over five hundred years.

The pub originated as an ale and cider parlour in 1485 and has retained its traditional atmosphere despite increasing popularity. Inside, there are dark timber beams, panelled walls, settles and wing chairs, and traditional bar games such as dominoes and cribbage are played.

To cope with extra trade during the busy summer months an adjoining barn has recently been converted into an additional bar.

THE OLD BULL
INKBERROW, HEREFORD AND WORCESTER

Located half-way between Worcester and Stratford-upon-Avon, Inkberrow has a village green surrounded by a mixture of half-timbered and mellow brick houses. At one end is The Old Bull, a three-storey sixteenth-century building that may have been a barn originally before becoming an alehouse.

The pub has three claims to fame, two of these, however, are somewhat doubtful. The first suggests that King Charles II stayed here after fleeing from the battle of Worcester in 1651; the second that William Shakespeare lodged at the inn on the way to Worcester to collect his marriage licence. Its third claim to fame is as the model for 'The Bull' in the everlasting radio series *The Archers*, evidence for this being provided by the press cuttings and signed photographs of the cast that cover the walls of the bar.

THE GOAT'S HEAD
ABBOTTS BROMLEY,
STAFFORDSHIRE

The seventeenth-century Goat's Head, one of many fine black-and-white half-timbered buildings in Abbotts Bromley, stands opposite a six-sided timber butter cross, indicating that this was once a market-place. Trading at the cross is recorded as early as the fourteenth century, although the present building, like the inn, dates from the seventeenth century.

The village is the scene of the famous Horn Dance each September when men in Tudor costume bearing sets of antlers on their shoulders dance their way round the local farms accompanied by a jester, hobby-horse and musicians. The purpose of the dance is uncertain although it has been suggested that it is a means of marking the parish boundaries or 'beating the bounds'. The antlers, which have been carbon dated to the eleventh century, hang in the church for the rest of the year.

THE WHITE HART
BOUTH, CUMBRIA

A typical country inn set at the bottom of Grizedale Forest between lakes Windermere and Coniston Water. The White Hart has been an inn for many years and the old 'hooker' ring, the tying-up point for the coaches that used to halt here on their way to London, is still fixed to the wall.

The walls are four feet thick in places and the bar floors are made from large pieces of Coniston slab slate. Inside the pub is a remarkable collection of stuffed animals that seem to occupy every square inch of space. All the creatures from wood, forest, hedge and meadow appear to be represented, including a badger, fox, stoat, weasel and hedgehog, all with glassy eyes focused sharply on the pub's customers.

THE MASON'S ARMS
KNOWSTONE, DEVON

Knowstone is on a typically hilly and winding Devon lane near the southern edge of Exmoor. The neatly thatched thirteenth-century pub is directly opposite the church which, in the nineteenth century, had a somewhat eccentric vicar. It was said that he hired a gang of thugs to intimidate parishioners who upset him or did not attend church and that he eventually died during a fit of extreme rage.

The Mason's Arms seems to epitomize the old English country pub where time stands still and all troubles are left outside. The rustic furniture, stone floors, antique farm tools, old bottles hanging from the beams, and open fire complete with bread oven all blend together in perfect harmony, and there are enough games to keep one happy for hours.

Plenty of rucksack-carrying visitors stop here as the pub is on the route of a long-distance walk across Dartmoor and Exmoor.

THE FALKLAND ARMS
GREAT TEW, OXFORDSHIRE

Great Tew was declared to be of 'outstanding interest' by the Department of the Environment in 1978 and a considerable amount of work has since been done to preserve this charming village of thatched and stone-roofed honey-coloured cottages. The pub is named after Lord Falkland who lived in the manor house in the seventeenth century.

The interior of The Falkland Arms is entirely in keeping with the rest of the village and has partly panelled stone walls, stripped tables and flagstone floors. One can experiment with over forty different kinds of snuff or even purchase a ready-filled clay pipe to smoke while participating in the traditional pub games of shove-halfpenny, dominoes, skittles and darts.

WELD ARMS
EAST LULWORTH, DORSET

A little way inland from the dramatic geological formation of Lulworth Cove, East Lulworth is far quieter than its coastal neighbour, even during the height of summer. The Weld Arms is a simple, whitewashed building, its porches enhanced by flowering clematis and its thatched roof overgrown with moss producing a subtle blend of browns and greens.

The inn was named after the Weld family whose nearby castle, set in six hundred acres of woodland, was unfortunately gutted by fire in 1929. The family chapel of St Mary in the grounds of the castle was the first Roman Catholic church built with royal permission after the Reformation.

THE WISE MAN INN
WEST STAFFORD, DORSET

The thatched roof of The Wise Man is decorated with cleverly fashioned straw birds and the façade adorned with old farming implements such as yolks and flails.

Set among the creepers that cover much of the exterior is the inn sign, which depicts a judge deep in thought. Further along the façade is a doggerel attributed to Thomas Hardy, although judging by its content this seems rather unlikely:

> I trust no wise man will
>   condemn
> A cup of genuine now and
>   then.
> When you're faint your spirits
>   low,
> Your string relaxed t'will
>   bend your bow,
> Brace your drumhead, make
>   you tight,
> Wind up your watch and put
>   you right.

NEW INN
CLOVELLY, DEVON

One of England's show villages, Clovelly remains refreshingly unspoilt despite its popularity. There is, however, little room for development as it plunges down a narrow cobbled street to the sea, the only traffic being pedestrians and the sledges that are used to haul goods up and down the hill.

The New Inn stands almost at the top of the hill, aptly named Steep Street, and from its enclosed terrace commands a stunning view over the rooftops. It is strategically placed to offer succour to those who, on their last legs after the ascent, may need fortification before facing the final trudge up to the hill-top car-park.

A noisy tradition is still carried on by the village children on Shrove Tuesday: they drag tin cans up and down the cobbles to scare off the Devil before Lent.

THE RED LION
AVEBURY, WILTSHIRE

The village of Avebury is completely encompassed by its neolithic stone circle and The Red Lion stands almost at the centre. The monument dates back to about 2,400 BC and is therefore older than Stonehenge. It consists of an outer ring of huge stones, some of which weigh up to sixty tons, flanked by earthworks, and two inner rings formed from smaller stones, many of which are missing, although their places have been marked by concrete posts.

The inn is L-shaped, beautifully thatched and half-timbered, and though substantially altered over the years, it does retain a seventeenth-century well in what is now the dining-room.

Avebury is one of several important ancient sites on the Marlborough Downs including Silbury Hill and West Kennett Long Barrow.

THE PLOUGH INN
KELMSCOT, OXFORDSHIRE

Kelmscot's inn is a small unpretentious house composed of several cottages that have been amalgamated over the years. Although well off the beaten track it attracts many visitors.

This straggling village on the upper reaches of the Thames is famous as the home of the poet and designer William Morris who lived at Kelmscott Manor, an Elizabethan mansion that has now been restored as a museum and contains examples of his wallpaper and furniture. Morris died in 1896 and is buried in the church a little way from The Plough.

BOTTLE AND GLASS
BINFIELD HEATH, OXFORDSHIRE

Binfield Heath lies in a network of wooded lanes to the west of the river Thames between Henley and Sonning. The sixteenth-century Bottle and Glass is a near-perfect example of the English country pub, with gleaming whitewashed walls interspaced with black timbers and an impeccably neat thatched roof. The interior is equally enchanting; the temptation to over-modernize has been firmly resisted and scrubbed tables still stand on old flagstone floors as they have for centuries.

It is likely that the pub's name originated in the mid-eighteenth century when glasses first came into general use as drinking vessels, the sign acting as an advertisement for the latest 'technology'.

The pub once had extensive stabling as it was situated on an old pack-horse route, a track that is now a public bridleway.

BEWICKE ARMS
HALLATON, LEICESTERSHIRE

The Bewicke Arms is one of three pubs in this attractively laid out village. It stands opposite the green where a conical-shaped butter cross indicates that a market was once held here.

Every Easter Monday, Hallaton stages a 'bottle kicking' contest between the village team and one from neighbouring Medbourne. The 'bottles' are in fact small beer-filled kegs that have to be carried over the opponent village's boundary. The event is almost certainly derived from pagan ritual and goes back many years in its present form. It can take hours for the result to be known as the barrel disappears for ages at a time under a heaving mass of bodies. After the contest the winner is chaired back to the butter cross where the cask is drained, celebrations then carry on with a vengeance in the pub.

Before the contest, a huge hare pie is provided and distributed by the vicar.

THE GEORGE INN
VERNHAM DEAN, HAMPSHIRE

The seventeenth-century ground floor of The George Inn is built of alternate courses of brick and flint supported by weathered timbers, while the tiled roof undulates gracefully above the windows of the later, brick upper storey. Inside, a homely and welcoming atmosphere prevails, aided by a huge log fire in the inglenook fireplace and by the comfortable chairs.

The village, which has a fine Jacobean house, Vernham Manor, is to the east of a Roman road known as Chute Causeway, which once linked Winchester and Marlborough. The section of the Causeway close to the village is said to have been haunted since the outbreak of plague that swept the country during the reign of Charles II.

THE RED LION
WEOBLEY, HEREFORD AND WORCESTER

The picturesque village of Weobley is filled with black-and-white half-timbered houses of which The Red Lion is one. The inn dates back to the fourteenth century and has plenty of charm and character as befits a building of its age.

A little way up from The Red Lion in the middle of the street is a rose garden that was once the site of the old market-place.

The famous red and white Hereford beef cattle are said to have been first bred here in the eighteenth century, by a villager named Benjamin Tomkins.

TAN HILL INN
TAN HILL, NORTH YORKSHIRE

To walkers of the Pennine Way the Tan Hill Inn must appear as a tantalizing mirage in a desert of heather-clad moorland. Having tramped over the rugged Yorkshire Dales, to come across England's highest pub provides an unexpected but very welcome watering hole. The pub, 1,732 feet above sea-level, was built in 1737 and catered for the miners who dug for coal on the bleak, desolate hills. They have long since disappeared but the unmarked shafts still offer a hazard to ramblers. The pub really comes alive each May when a sheep fair is held here.

A radio telephone is the pub's only link with the outside world, electricity is provided by generator and gas is bottled.

EIGHT BELLS
BOLNEY, WEST SUSSEX

The main London to Brighton road bypasses the now quiet village of Bolney. The sixteenth-century Eight Bells stands on a slight hill directly opposite Bolney's church with its Norman nave and chancel. Traditionally the village pub and church are often linked; the vicar sometimes sold 'church ales' on feast-days and holidays, the derived income contributing to the church funds. One of the first landlords of the Eight Bells was the churchwarden who certainly did ensure that his parishioners should 'not thirst after righteousness'!

The pub has a most attractive three-dimensional sign with eight bells, the number that hang in the church, enclosed in a wrought-iron frame.

MARKET CROSS INN
ALFRISTON, EAST SUSSEX

Alfriston stands where an ancient ridgeway crosses the River Cuckmere, and has been the site of a settlement since early Saxon times. The river and complex network of paths that criss-cross the South Downs were used in the early nineteenth century by the notorious Alfriston Gang, a band of smugglers whose leader, Stanton Collins, lived in the Market Cross.

Now subtitled 'Ye Olde Smugglers', there is a story that Collins once hid eight of his men up a chimney during a raid by excise officers. A pair of cutlasses hanging over the inglenook fireplace serve as a reminder of those wilder days. Collins was, however, finally transported to Australia for sheep stealing.

HOLLY BUSH
LITTLE LEIGH, CHESHIRE

The thatched, timber-frame-and-red-brick Holly Bush blends so well with the working farm in whose yard it stands that it can be difficult to locate, especially as its unostentatious sign is partially hidden in the tree after which the pub is named.

Inside, time seems to have stood still. Beer is served in the traditional way from the taproom doorway, and the highly polished tables grouped round an open fire give the atmosphere of a private gathering of friends.

ROYAL OAK INN
WINSFORD, SOMERSET

To many people Winsford is the perfect example of a typical English village, and the thatched Royal Oak the ideal country inn. Beautifully located on the eastern fringes of Exmoor, Winsford marks the confluence of the Rivers Winn and Exe. The village has eight bridges, several of which were built for the pack-horses that carried local wool south to Exeter and Tiverton.

The inn probably originated in the twelfth century as a farmhouse that began supplying home-brewed ale to travellers, the custom growing as the traffic increased. An infamous local highwayman named Tom Faggus who robbed the inn's visitors was incorporated by Blackmore into his famous novel, *Lorna Doone*.

FLEECE INN

BRETFORTON, HEREFORD AND WORCESTER

The National Trust acquired the Fleece in 1978 when it was bequeathed to them by Miss Lola Taplin, whose family had owned it for generations. The medieval building was a farm until converted into a beerhouse in 1848. In those days the pub had its own brewery and all three parlours were served from one hatch in the hall.

Ale was stored in casks away from the bars to keep it cool and this is the origin of the 'taprooms' found in many Victorian pubs. The original system has given way to hand pumps, but apart from a serving bar near the hatch the whole of the interior has changed little over the years. When the pub was given to the Trust, all the furnishings were included and there are many antiques, particularly fine is a forty-eight-piece set of Stuart pewter.

THE DRUNKEN DUCK

HAWKSHEAD, CUMBRIA

High above Hawkshead at a remote crossroads on the road to Ambleside is The Drunken Duck inn. The pub is some four hundred years old and was formerly known as the Barngate Inn.

Its present name dates back to Victorian times, when a landlady found six ducks, apparently dead, outside the door. She had nearly finished plucking them before she noticed signs of life and realized that the poor creatures had been drinking from a leaking beer barrel and were actually drunk. As they had been stripped of their plumage the landlady knitted woollen jackets for them until their feathers grew again.

WATERSIDE PUBS

Set amongst lush greenery on the banks of the Thames, The Trout at Godstow has for centuries been a satisfying and welcoming sight for generations of Oxford under-graduates, and the ruins of a Benedictine nunnery for which it was originally a guest-house can still be seen in the meadow on the other side of the river. Built of mellow stone, the picturesque White Hart at Stopham in West Sussex lies next to a fourteenth-century bridge under whose seven graceful arches the River Arun slowly meanders creating a peaceful setting that is a paradise for anglers. England's countryside, rich in rivers and canals, boasts many such charming and historic waterside pubs.

Before the road and bridge network became established, rivers and estuaries had to be crossed by ferry. The ferries developed into important meeting-places, and the ferryman would probably offer his passengers a glass of ale in return for the news they brought from the outside world. The pubs that developed at these ancient crossing points – often in the ferryman's cottage – are some of the oldest in the country; Ye Olde Ferry Boat at Holywell, dates back to AD 968.

Boat, Ship, Navigation and Barge are just some of the pub names that reflect the great era of English canal-building. Most of the canals were built during the eighteenth century to provide a freight transport system for an increasingly industrial society. Like the coaching inns on the main trunk roads, the canal-side inns acted as trading-posts and mail collection and delivery centres for the men who worked the narrow boats. Water-borne freight traffic has become a thing of the past, but the pubs that once served the bargees remain to cater for the pleasure-boat trade that is now booming as silted-up canals are being cleared and more people are taking to the water for recreation.

High import duties imposed during the eighteenth century on various goods including spirits, tea and silks caused an upsurge of smuggling along England's coasts, particularly in the south and south-east where a lucrative illegal trade in brandy and rum prospered. Coastal pubs were often the haunt of smugglers and wreckers, and some, like the Royal Oak at Langstone and the Pilchard at Bigbury, were renowned for their smuggling associations, and even now retain much of their colourful atmosphere.

ANCHOR INN
BARCOMBE, EAST SUSSEX

The Anchor Inn enjoys a totally isolated position on the River Ouse about four miles from Lewes. It was built in 1790 and catered for the horse-drawn barges that travelled upstream from Newhaven until the advent of the railways caused the demise of water freight transport.

Towards the end of the nineteenth century the inn's licence was withdrawn when the landlord was caught using the Anchor as a base for smuggling. However, its licence has since been restored and the River Ouse is now a tranquil paradise for naturalists and anglers.

THE SHROPPIE FLY
AUDLEM, CHESHIRE

This unusually named pub occupies a late-eighteenth-century mill on the edge of the Shropshire Union Canal. Its name derives from the especially fast narrow boats, or fly boats, that were used to transport perishable goods by canal before the advent of the railways. There were several companies building fly boats along this section of the canal. The crane for winching cargo between the mill and the fly boats still stands just outside the pub.

One of the most exciting features of the pub is its bar, which is formed from a complete narrow boat that was somehow manoeuvred into place when the mill was restored and converted into a pub about fifteen years ago. Even with cranes to help this can have been no mean feat.

Audlem itself is an old small market town with a splendid Perpendicular church of red sandstone.

THE ROYAL OAK
LANGSTONE, HAMPSHIRE

Langstone stands on the edge of the creek that separates Hayling Island from the mainland. At high tide the sea laps at the wall in front of The Royal Oak, while at low water the acres of green slime and mud revealed are a favourite haunt of waders and other sea-birds. Identification of species while sitting in the pub's window-seats is made easier by the many prints of birds that hang around the walls.

The Langstone Gang was a well-known band of smugglers who ran the excise gauntlet to land their hauls of brandy here. They devised an ingenious system of towing their cargo to shore on submerged rafts so that, if challenged, no contraband would be found on board.

THE BOAT INN
STOKE BRUERNE, NORTHAMPTONSHIRE

The seventeenth-century thatched limestone cottages that now form The Boat Inn sit right on the tow-path of the Grand Union Canal next to some lock gates. This is a colourful corner, with brightly painted narrow boats moored outside the pub and on the opposite bank near the Waterways Museum.

Despite extensions through the years to cope with increasing trade, the bars retain the original stone floors and open fires. Traditional Northamptonshire skittles are played in a separate room and one could well find that throwing the oddly shaped ball or 'cheese', as it is called locally, is not as easy as it looks in the hands of a regular. The old stables have been converted into a tea-room ensuring that, even with England's odd licensing laws, refreshment is available at all times.

WHITE SWAN
BARNARD CASTLE, COUNTY DURHAM

Towering over the White Swan are the impressive ruins of a cliff-top castle built by Bernard de Baliol in the twelfth century to guard a ford across the River Tees.

The solidly built pub appears to be part of the sixteenth-century bridge that replaced the ford. As a defence against winter floods the pub's sturdy walls have few windows, so no views are offered of the river or castle. A friendlier atmosphere prevails inside, however, where racks of antique plates are hung on the polished panelled walls.

Barnard Castle has one of the best museums in the country, the Bowes Museum. Housed in a nineteenth-century mansion built in the style of a French château, it contains a magnificent collection of European art and furniture.

THE FERRY
BABLOCKHYTHE, OXFORDSHIRE

During Saxon times, Bablockhythe was an important crossing-point of the river Thames and lay on an ancient track that linked the settlements of Oxford and Witney. There has been a ferry across the river here since AD 950, and it still operates today, often carrying visitors to and from the pub.

Right on the water's edge, The Ferry was built in the early nineteenth century, although it has been substantially rebuilt since. Some kind of pub or inn has occupied the site for centuries, and local ecclesiastical records indicate that there was a monks' rest-house here during the early Middle Ages.

The pub once catered for the bargees of the nineteenth century, but now serves the pleasure-boat trade on this delightful stretch of the river.

BUTT AND OYSTER
CHELMONDISTON, SUFFOLK

A 'butt' is the local name for a flounder. This popular sixteenth-century waterside pub overlooks Buttermans Bay, part of the wide River Orwell that flows from Ipswich into the North Sea. The large cargo vessels that negotiate the river on their way to and from the docks at Ipswich can be watched in comfort on settles through the pub's bay windows.

Huge black sailing barges are beached on the silt at low tide, dwarfing the countless smaller craft moored here. This is very much a sailor's pub and the talk has probably changed little from the days when it was patronized by the bargees of the last century.

RASHLEIGH INN
POLKERRIS, CORNWALL

The Rashleigh Inn is idyllically situated in its own quiet sandy cove, surrounded by some of the most attractive coastal scenery in Cornwall, which can be fully appreciated from the pub's terrace or from a huge bay window that looks out over the sea.

The inn is named after the Rashleigh family who lived at Menabilly, a seventeenth-century house that has more recently been the home of novelist Daphne du Maurier.

RAMSHOLT ARMS
RAMSHOLT, SUFFOLK

Set in glorious isolation, the Ramsholt Arms is right on the shoreline of the River Debden next to an old barge quay. The old cargo boats have now disappeared to be replaced by pleasure craft of all shapes and sizes.

Cars are discouraged from venturing down to the water's edge and the air is filled only with the cries of gulls, curlews and other sea-birds. The pub is simply but attractively furnished and one can peacefully sit and watch the world drift by through the picture windows or from the paved terrace outside.

THE BARGE
HONEY STREET,
WILTSHIRE

The Kennet and Avon Canal flows through beautiful downland countryside, linking Newbury with Bath. Completed in the early nineteenth century, it is fifty-seven miles long and took twenty-four years to build. One of the most interesting sections of the waterway is at Honey Street where a wharf was built in 1811 with a curious weather-boarded clock tower – now minus its clock.

A short distance away is The Barge, built to serve the boat-builders from the wharf and passing bargees. Originally it had a shop and bakery and probably also brewed its own beer for a time. In 1858 a fire started in the stables killing nearly all the barge horses kept there, and gutting the inn. There was no loss of human life, although a local newspaper reported at the time that several men had fallen drunk into the canal after raiding the cellars, which had survived the blaze.

NAPTON BRIDGE INN
NAPTON ON THE HILL,
WARWICKSHIRE

Napton Hill stands several hundred feet above the surrounding flat landscape and from its summit, which has been occupied since Saxon times, seven counties can be seen. The Oxford Canal makes a sharp detour to avoid the hill and next to one of the bridges that crosses this stretch of the water is the Napton Bridge Inn. It was built some two hundred years ago as a changing post for the barge horses that hauled narrow boats along the canal and gradually became a pub by the end of the nineteenth century.

The canal is now busier than ever, and a colourful assortment of boats are always tied up outside the pub. One of the stables has been turned into a bar where traditional skittles are played.

BOAT INN
GNOSALL, STAFFORDSHIRE

Originally a small cottage, the Boat has been an inn ever since the opening of this section of the Shropshire Union Canal in the 1830s. The stables and hayloft, such important parts of all canal-side pubs in the days of horse-drawn barges, have now been incorporated into the existing building.

'Boat', 'Navigation', 'Ship', and 'Narrowboat' are quite common pub names in the Midlands, giving some indication of the complex network of waterways that threads its way through the region. With the advent of rail freight transport, canal traffic declined, but recently revived interest has led to much restoration work by enthusiasts. Neglected, weed-clogged channels have been reopened and pubs like the Boat are once again thriving on trade from passing narrow boats.

WHITE HART
STOPHAM, WEST SUSSEX

The White Hart stands next to a fourteenth-century bridge that spans the River Arun, both bridge and pub being built of the same mellow stone. Visitors to the White Hart can enjoy the sight and sound of the water flowing lazily through the bridge's seven graceful arches or wander along the bank to where the Arun meets the River Rother. This area is extremely popular with anglers.

The interior of the pub is quite unspoilt and its three bars are simply furnished. As befits its location, the White Hart has a good reputation for the fresh fish served in its candle-lit restaurant.

THE ROSE REVIVED
NEWBRIDGE, OXFORDSHIRE

Newbridge is a serious contender for the title of the oldest bridge across the Thames. It was rebuilt in the fifteenth century by the landlord of the inn that is now called The Rose Revived, but was then known as the Chequers.

Exterior rebuilding in the 1930s obscures the true age of the inn whose character is better revealed by the interior with its low ceilings and original timbers. There are several theories as to how the inn was given its strange and romantic name. The most logical seems to be that it was originally called The Rose, was renamed The Crown by a new landlord, but that a successor chose to return to the older title. The inn sign, however, depicts another theory: Oliver Cromwell, who had stopped at the inn for refreshment during the Civil War, apparently noticed that the rose he was wearing on his tunic had wilted and placed it in a tankard of ale, where it did indeed revive.

THE HORSESHOE
LLANYBLODWEL, SHROPSHIRE

Despite the Welsh name, translated it means 'village of flowers', Llanyblodwel is in fact a mile from the Welsh border. The Horseshoe is a rambling sixteenth-century black-and-white building which stands next to an ancient bridge over the River Tanat. It was only recently that ownership passed from the family that had run the pub for over three hundred years.

On a hill above the river is the village church, which bears the marks left by an eccentric vicar in the nineteenth century who rebuilt the church adding a peculiar cigar-shaped tower. He was also responsible for the curious turrets and gables on what was once the village school.

THE TROUT
GODSTOW, OXFORDSHIRE

The Trout is one of the most picturesque of the Thameside pubs, but its proximity to Oxford means it is also one of the busiest, particularly in summer.

It stands next to a bridge and weir opposite the ruins of a Benedictine nunnery, for which The Trout was originally the guest-house. After the dissolution of the monasteries in the 1530s the nunnery became a private house. It was sacked, however, during the Civil War and stone from the ruins was used when the guest-house was later enlarged to become an inn.

Godstow is associated with Henry II's mistress, Fair Rosamund, who was allegedly poisoned at the nunnery by the jealous Queen Eleanor. It was on this stretch of river that Lewis Carroll first told the story of Alice in Wonderland to three girls, one of whom was Alice Liddell, the model for the story's heroine.

THE TROUT
LECHLADE, GLOUCESTERSHIRE

The Trout, which possesses two miles of fishing rights, stands next to St John's bridge, where the River Leach flows into the Thames. About half a mile to the west is Lechlade, the highest navigable point on the Thames for motor cruisers.

In the thirteenth century an Augustinian hospital occupied the site, later a priory and eventually an inn which until 1704 was known as the St John the Baptist's Head. Some remains of the priory can still be seen in the pub's garden.

The statue of Old Father Thames, which used to sit at the river's source, has been moved to St John's lock, just across the bridge, to protect it from vandalism.

THE GOLDEN BALL
HEATON WITH OXCLIFFE, LANCASHIRE

Notices by the roadside warn of possible flooding at high tide as one approaches The Golden Ball, an isolated pub situated on the water's edge of the tidal River Lune.

In the snug and cosy bars, pictures of some of the tall ships that once used the river give a clue as to the origin of the Golden Ball's alternative name, Snatchems. This was once a hunting-ground for the press-gangs, which, as their name implies, coerced men into service at sea against their will. The gang's job was made easier by the drunken state of the pub's customers who often did not wake up until well out to sea the following day.

PILCHARD INN
BIGBURY-ON-SEA, DEVON

Burgh Island is a three-hundred-yard walk across the sands from the mainland and perched on its rocks well above the reach of the sea is the Pilchard Inn. This ancient storm-beaten smugglers' haunt, which dates back to 1336, is cut off for up to eight hours by each tide. Visitors who suddenly become aware of the advancing waters need not fear for the Pilchard has a unique vehicle, a motorized 'bus on stilts', that carries people safely above the level of the waves back to their cars on the mainland.

The atmosphere inside the inn is enhanced by the use of old ships' lanterns for lighting and by blazing log fires in winter. This is really the best season to visit the Pilchard, when all the holiday crowds have gone and it stands alone as it has done for centuries.

MASTER BUILDER'S HOUSE HOTEL
BUCKLERS HARD, HAMPSHIRE

Lord Nelson is reputed to have said that the *Agamemnon*, which he captained in 1783, was his favourite ship. Launched at Bucklers Hard in 1781, it had been built by Henry Adams, who was responsible during his lifetime for the construction of over forty ships. Adams's house has been run as a hotel since 1926 and, inside, his workroom has been re-created complete with charts, drawings and models much as it would have been while he worked there.

Bucklers Hard was an ideal location for ship-building being close to the New Forest with its ample supplies of oak and right on the Beaulieu River. The great width of the main street allowed whole tree trunks to be stacked and dried before being rolled down to the water's edge. The hamlet is now preserved as a maritime museum.

YE OLDE LEATHERNE BOTTLE
GORING, OXFORDSHIRE

Goring, which is situated where the river Thames has worn a gentle gorge between the Chilterns and the Berkshire Downs, has been an important crossing point of the river since prehistoric times and links two ancient tracks, the Ridgeway and the Icknield Way.

About a mile from the village, well hidden at the foot of a steeply wooded hill and overlooking one of the most picturesque parts of the river, is Ye Olde Leatherne Bottle. The oldest parts of the inn date from the sixteenth century and some original stonework is still visible. The bar runs through three adjoining rooms with many window seats where one can sit and watch the river drift by.

ANCHOR INN
SEATOWN, DORSET

Seatown and the Anchor Inn are dominated by Golden Cap, which, at 617 feet, is the highest point on England's South Coast. To the east lies Chesil Beach, an immense mass of shingle several miles long and up to 150 feet wide, whose shape is constantly being altered by the tides.

The Dorset coastal path virtually passes through the Anchor's bars, which have low, white, boarded ceilings and walls hung with sailing pictures.

Although pleasant in summer, the pub is perhaps best appreciated out of season after a windy tramp along the pebble beach.

THE PANDORA INN
MYLOR BRIDGE, CORNWALL

The Pandora enjoys an idyllic setting on the shore of Restronguet Creek, one of the many inlets radiating from the Carrick Roads, Falmouth's natural harbour. The pub has been licensed since the fourteenth century and is one of the oldest in Cornwall.

In the rambling flagstoned bar the raised fireplace is a precaution against flooding during exceptionally high tides. Although modernized to cope with its popularity, the inn has retained many original features and one is left in no doubt as to its great age.

The name has nautical connections: HMS *Pandora* was the ship sent to chase Fletcher Christian and his crew after the famous mutiny on Captain Bligh's ship the *Bounty*.

YE OLDE FERRY BOAT
HOLYWELL, CAMBRIDGESHIRE

Situated on the banks of the tidal Great Ouse, the thatched Ferry Boat, one of the oldest pubs in England, originated in AD 968 as an alehouse. There was a ferry across this stretch of the river until the 1930s which supplied much of the inn's trade and gave it its name.

Inside the pub some ancient bog oak beams are still visible in the low ceilings, and one can watch the river through the many tiny old windows that help retain the character of this charming building.

The Ferry Boat was popular with bargees during the last century, and today visitors still arrive at the inn by boat. Reeds growing along this section of the Ouse are used in wickerwork and basket-making, and during July can be seen being cut and laid out to dry along the banks.

MOTHER SHIPTON INN
KNARESBOROUGH, NORTH YORKSHIRE

Knaresborough stands on a sandstone cliff around the foot of which curls the River Nidd. Many caves have formed in the soft rock, and according to legend it was in one of these that Mother Shipton was born in 1488. She became known as a witch and prophetess; her prophecies were always written in rhyme and covered a wide range of topics including the accession of Elizabeth I, Sir Walter Raleigh's voyages to America and his discovery of tobacco and potatoes:

> from whence he shall bring,
> a herb and a root,
> that all men shall suit,
> and please both the
> ploughman and King.

Parts of the Mother Shipton Inn, which is just infront of Mother Shipton's cave, date from the mid-seventeenth century when the building was used as a farmhouse; it became an inn during the last century.

Pubs with Literary Associations

Six centuries ago, Geoffrey Chaucer wrote of the landlord of The Tabard in London, where his odd assortment of pilgrims gathered at the start of their journey in *The Canterbury Tales*, 'our host gave us great welcome, everyone was given a place and supper was begun. He served the finest victuals you could think, the wine was strong and we were glad to drink.'

Literature and the English inn have long enjoyed a close association. Many of our greatest writers, poets and diarists have at one time or another sojourned at or written about some of the most colourful inns in the country, and through their accounts can be glimpsed fascinating scenes of pub life at different periods in history. For instance, as the standard of road and transport improved during the seventeenth century, chroniclers of English life such as Samuel Pepys were more easily able to travel away from London into the provinces and record their experiences for posterity. The Chequers in Fowlmere proudly displays a segment of Pepys's *Diary* – a mine of information about seventeenth-century English life – which refers to his stay there in 1660, when he dined on a 'breast of veal roasted'. On a journey from Salisbury in 1688 he mentions in his *Diary* that 'with great difficulty [we] came about ten at night to a little inn, where we were fain to go into a room where a pedlar was in bed, and made him rise, and there wife and I lay, and in a truckle bed Betty Turner and Deb Willett . . . . Up and found our beds good but lousy, which made us merry.'

Dr Johnson, that eminent eighteenth-century commentator, spoke in glowing terms about the inn thus, 'There is no private house . . . in which people can enjoy themselves so well, as at a capital tavern.' He continues on the same theme, as reported by Boswell, 'You are sure you are welcome; and the more noise you make, the more trouble you give, the more good things you call for, the wellcomer you are . . . . No, Sir; there is nothing which has yet been contrived by man, by which so much happiness is produced as by a good tavern or inn.'

Charles Dickens travelled a good deal in England while researching his novels, many of which include brilliant observations of nineteenth-century tavern scenes based on

THE SWAN
GRASMERE, CUMBRIA

William Wordsworth spent fourteen years in Grasmere and described it as 'the lovliest spot that man hath ever found'. His best known house was Dove Cottage, just down the road from The Swan, an old posting house that was affectionately mentioned in his poem, 'The Waggoner'.

When Sir Walter Scott stayed with the Wordsworths he apparently found their hospitality lacking in certain respects and was forced to make furtive visits to the inn for regular 'fortifiers'. His deception came to an embarrassing end when the two men arrived at The Swan to hire a pony for a trip up the fells; the landlord expressed surprise at seeing Wordsworth's friend so much earlier than his usual time.

the inns he patronized. He used one of his haunts, The Waggon and Horses at Beckhampton, as a model for the inn in 'The Bagman's Story' in *The Pickwick Papers.* In the story Tom Smart, a commercial traveller, arrives at a roadside inn on a rainy wind-swept evening. Tom describes the inn as 'a comfortable-looking place though, for there was a strong cheerful light in the bar-window, which shed a bright ray across the road, and even lighted up the hedge on the other side; and there was a red flickering light in the opposite window ... which intimated that a rousing fire was blazing.' Very soon Tom has settled into the inn 'his slippered feet on the fender, and his back to the open door, he saw a charming prospect of the bar reflected in the glass over the chimney-piece, with delightful rows of green bottles and gold labels, together with jars of pickles and preserves, and cheeses and boiled hams, and rounds of beef, arranged on shelves in the most tempting and delicious array.'

One of the most famous inns in English literature, whether fact or fiction, is the Jamaica Inn. Daphne du Maurier chose this isolated granite building high on Bodmin Moor in Cornwall as the setting for her novel of the same name, based on the vagabonds and smugglers who frequented it during the eighteenth century. Another ancient pub with strong literary connections is The Mermaid at Rye, where Russell Thorndyke set his *Dr Syn* novels about a vicar who indulged in a little smuggling.

'The quaintest, most old-world inn on the river ... a story book appearance while inside it is still more once-upon-a-timeyfied' was how Jerome K. Jerome, author of *Three Men in a Boat,* described the Barley Mow at Clifton Hampden. He spent many hours contemplating the passing river Thames from here, and it has been claimed that he wrote much of his famous book on the premises. This, and other such claims, may be exaggerated, but that the comings and goings of a pub's clientele and the conversations overheard at the bar must often have served as inspiration cannot be doubted.

> But lo, the old inn, and the lights, and the fire,
> And the fiddler's old tune and the shuffling of feet;
> Soon for us shall be quiet and rest and desire,
> And to-morrow's uprising to deeds shall be sweet.
>
> (William Morris)

RHYDSPENCE INN
WHITNEY, HEREFORD AND WORCESTER

Just twenty yards from the Welsh border, the Rhydspence is a fourteenth-century half-timbered building commanding impressive views over the Wye valley and the hills beyond. The interior is full of low, beamed ceilings and cushioned benches that surround a big stone hearth.

Between 1865 and 1872 diarist Revd Francis Kilvert was curate at nearby Clyro church just across the border. While passing the Rhydspence one night he noticed 'the English inn still ablaze with light with the song of revellers'. Wales, however, was firmly teetotal at the time.

MORRITT ARMS
GRETA BRIDGE, COUNTY DURHAM

This stone coaching inn, formerly known as The George, is beautifully situated on the banks of the River Greta. Its location seemingly inspired many of its residents to take up a pen or a brush, for several leading writers and artists have lodged here, including Dickens, Cotman and Turner. Dickens and his illustrator, Hablot Browne, stayed here in 1838 after a two-day journey from London on the Carlisle coach. They arrived in deep snow *en route* for Barnard Castle where Dickens was going to research *Nicholas Nickleby*.

The present name of the inn comes from Squire Morritt of Rokeby House, which is just under a mile away. Rokeby was painted by Turner and featured in a poem by Sir Walter Scott, a great friend of Morritt's.

THE WAGGON AND HORSES
BECKHAMPTON, WILTSHIRE

Charles Dickens must have been impressed by the character of this thatched Tudor coaching inn because he featured it in 'The Bagman's Story' in *The Pickwick Papers*. The story involved a commercial traveller called Tom Smart who stays the night at the inn which is run by a buxom, widowed landlady. After several glasses of hot punch and a good meal Tom goes to bed, but spends a disturbed night during which an old chair in his room assumes human form and advises him of the best way to secure the widow's affections. On waking, Tom carries out the chair's advice and soon he is installed in the comfortable inn on a more permanent basis.

The Waggon and Horses lies close to the prehistoric mound of Silbury Hill and was built with material from the stone circles at Avebury. It was well known as a halt for freight waggons on the route from London to Bath and had its own smithy, and stables.

THE SWAN INN
SOUTHROP,
GLOUCESTERSHIRE

Southrop is a typical Cotswold village with charming houses and cottages overlooked by a Norman and Early English church. The Swan stands at one corner of the tiny green, its walls absolutely covered in creepers. This cosy village pub dates back to 1645 and has a mixed history – at one time it was the premises of the local coffin maker.

John Keble, the poet and clergyman, lived in the nearby Old Vicarage and is supposed to have frequented The Swan on occasions. He became non-resident curate of the two churches in neighbouring Eastleach in 1815, and organized regular weekend reading parties at the Vicarage for students from Oxford; these discussions proved influential in the formation of the Oxford Movement. After his death in 1866 an Oxford college was built and named in honour of Keble.

TOWER BANK ARMS
NEAR SAWREY, CUMBRIA

The small black-and-white cottage pub is owned and run by the National Trust, which also administers the house directly behind it, Hill Top Farm. This was the home of Beatrix Potter and was where she wrote and illustrated many of her delightful children's books.

In one of her books, *Jemima Puddle-Duck*, there is a drawing of the pub with a butcher's horse-drawn cart in front. Little seems to have changed since her day apart from the horse being replaced by a motor vehicle.

The pub's interior is traditional and simply furnished with settles on the slate floor and a big, wood-burning cooking range.

BLACK BULL
HAWORTH,
WEST YORKSHIRE

Haworth, the home of the
Brontë family, is almost as
famous as Stratford-upon-Avon
as a place of literary pilgrimage.
The Revd Patrick Brontë
brought his family to live in the
parsonage at Haworth in 1820
and it is now kept as a museum.

At the top of the steep and
cobbled main street is the Black
Bull, with its gritstone walls
blackened by years of smoke
pollution from the local woollen
mills. The tall mill chimneys no
longer exist and the air is now
clean, but the Industrial
Revolution has left its mark on
Haworth as on all the Pennine
villages.

Branwell Brontë spent many
hours drinking at the Black Bull
and eventually, in 1845, his
consumption of alcohol and
opium killed him. His sister
Emily caught a chill at his
funeral and died just ten days
later, not living to receive the
acclaim given to her novel
Wuthering Heights.

FAUCONBERG ARMS
COXWOLD,
NORTH YORKSHIRE

This seventeenth-century inn
is named after the Earl of
Fauconberg who lived at nearby
Newburgh Hall and was married
to Cromwell's daughter, Mary.
There is a belief that Mary
brought her father's body to the
Hall after his death in 1658 and
that it still lies undiscovered in a
bricked-up vault.

Across the cobbled street from
the Fauconberg Arms is the
church where Laurence Sterne,
author of *Tristram Shandy*, was
the vicar from 1760 until his
death eight years later. The
parsonage, that has since been
called Shandy Hall, is open to
the public and some rooms there
have been kept as they were in
his day.

From the outside the pub does
not look very old, but once
inside, the huge beams and
joists, flagstone floors and great
fireplace retain the atmosphere
of the late eighteenth century
when the pub was completely
restored.

ANCIENT UNICORN
BOWES, COUNTY DURHAM

Bowes Academy and its headmaster, William Shaw, were Dickens's models for Dotheby's Hall and the cruel Wackford Squeers in his novel *Nicholas Nickleby*. The building still stands in the village today.

The Ancient Unicorn is a sixteenth-century coaching inn that was once an important stage on the York to Carlisle run. It is said that Dickens met a local farmer here who tried to dissuade the author from sending a child to the school. In order to gain access to the notorious boarding schools of the area, Dickens had assumed a false identity and had papers to say that he was acting for someone who wished their child to attend the Academy.

THE CHEQUERS
FOWLMERE, CAMBRIDGESHIRE

Samuel Pepys made regular journeys from London to visit the colleges of Cambridge University and his family home at Brampton near Huntingdon. He used a variety of routes and stayed at many inns along the way. Fowlmere was one hard day's ride from the capital and he dined and lodged at The Chequers on 24 February 1660, one day after his twenty-seventh birthday.

Pepys had begun his famous diary on 1 January that year and the entry for his evening at The Chequers mentions that he 'played cards until supper and then dined on breast of veal, roasted'.

The Chequers has in the past been a butcher's shop and a bakery, and at one stage functioned simultaneously as both an inn and a chapel of rest, thus being able to offer overnight accommodation to both the living and the dead!

THE MERMAID
RYE, EAST SUSSEX

Rye was originally one of the Cinque Ports but gradual silting has now left it some two miles inland.

The Mermaid was rebuilt in 1420, after a raid by the French reduced the old inn to ruins with the exception of the cellars. It has remained substantially unaltered through the years, possibly because it is situated on a narrow, cobbled hill that offers limited vehicular access.

Russell Thorndyke used The Mermaid as the setting for his *Dr Syn* novels, stories about a smuggling parson. It was a very apt choice of location because during the eighteenth century Rye was terrorized by the vicious Hawkhurst Gang, a band of smugglers who made The Mermaid their base. So tight was their grip on the area that the law was powerless to stop them and witnesses would not testify against them for fear of their lives.

Novelist Henry James lived in Rye from 1898 until his death in 1916 and was a regular visitor to the inn.

JAMAICA INN
BOLVENTOR, CORNWALL

Although now very much a tourist industry, Jamaica Inn has not lost the atmosphere that was immortalized by Daphne du Maurier in her novel of the same name.

On a dull day or at dusk, when the grey stone-and-slate building merges with the sky, one is easily transported back two hundred years ago to the days of the smugglers who frequented this lonely place. The inn was known by its present name as far back as the eighteenth century, possibly due to the lucrative local rum trade.

Jamaica Inn was a posting house on the wild and rough route across Bodmin Moor to west Cornwall, travellers having to share the warmth of the fire with rogues and villains who would probably follow their coach and hold it to ransom. That same fire is still kept burning all year round.

BELL INN
BURWASH, EAST SUSSEX

Burwash was an important centre of the iron industry in the seventeenth century when most of the country's ore came from the Weald. It was the home of Rudyard Kipling who lived at Bateman's, a house built by a Sussex ironmaster. He described this beautiful village, its Jacobean inn, the Bell, and the surrounding countryside in his novel *Puck of Pooks Hill*. Even though the pub's interior is now open-plan, the style and comfort found here have probably changed little since Kipling lived in the village.

BARLEY MOW
CLIFTON HAMPDEN, OXFORDSHIRE

A medieval cruck-framed building dating from 1350, the Barley Mow is perhaps best known for its connection with Jerome K. Jerome's book *Three Men in a Boat*, most of which he is supposed to have written in the pub. It is situated just a few yards from a Victorian bridge that crosses the Thames and one could easily imagine the rowing boat and its three passengers floating gently along on the current.

There is no question that Jerome visited the inn, even if he didn't write his book here, for he described it as 'the quaintest, most old-world inn on the river . . . a story book appearance, while inside it is still more once-upon-a-timeyfied'. It still fits this description and anyone of above average height will be stooping unless they retreat to the pretty gardens.

HAUNTED PUBS

Tom Busby, fresh from his hanging for the murder of his father-in-law, his head drooping and a hangman's noose still around his neck, is a regular at the Busby Stoop Inn in North Yorkshire, where the landlord thoughtfully keeps a chair reserved for this grim visitor. A young woman, abandoned at the altar, waits for her wedding breakfast at the Castle Inn in Derbyshire many centuries after she died of a broken heart.

The whole subject of the supernatural and paranormal is an emotive one. There are those who fervently believe in ghosts, but there are also the disbelievers who scorn the notion with equal passion. There are certainly many pubs in the land that claim to be haunted, and maybe even the most hardened sceptics among us should not reject their claims too hastily!

Soldiers are perhaps the most commonly seen ghosts, the English Civil War having produced a rich selection of Roundheads and Cavaliers. Oliver Cromwell's cousin, John Hampden, who met his death at the hands of Prince Rupert's cavalry early in the campaign, paces a room named in his honour at The Plough at Clifton Hampden.

The mysterious rattling of windows and banging of doors that are heard in many older pubs might be the work of a poltergeist, a noisy mischievous ghost that makes its presence felt by its unruly behaviour. The Bull at Long Melford has in the past felt the full force of such a spirit, but recent renovations and draught-proofing might be responsible for a noticeable reduction in the ghost's enthusiasm.

A pub's previous function sometimes helps to explain a strange apparition. The unfortunate leper stoned to death by the people of Thame in Oxfordshire, still haunts The Birdcage, serving as a grisly reminder of the building's previous role as prison and lock-up. While a visitor to The Talbot at Oundle might be surprised to see Mary Queen of Scots descending the main staircase, but her presence can be accounted for quite simply. When the inn was being rebuilt in 1626 a staircase was brought from nearby Fotheringay Castle to be installed in the inn. Mary had descended these very steps on her way to her execution in 1587.

BLACK HORSE
PLUCKLEY, KENT

The curiously shaped windows of the Black Horse are to be found on most of the cottages in the village. They were built this way to celebrate the escape of a member of a prominent local family, the Derings, through a similarly shaped window during the Civil War while fleeing from the Parliamentarians.

This is reputed to be one of the most haunted villages in the country, claiming at least twelve ghosts. The poltergeist that occupies the Black Horse is that of a girl called Jessie Brooks, killed by a ball in the skittle alley when the pub was located elsewhere in the village. She obligingly moved with the Black Horse when it transferred to its present location 150 years ago.

LORD CREWE ARMS
BLANCHLAND, NORTHUMBERLAND

The almost regimented neatness of Blanchland comes as a surprise after travelling over rough moorland and passing the huge, isolated Derwent Reservoir just above the village. Although most of the village was built in the eighteenth century, the basis of the community was an abbey founded in the twelfth century by Premonstratensian Canons, and many of the stone cottages are grouped in a square following the original layout of the abbey.

The inn was formed from the abbot's lodgings, guest-house and abbey kitchens. It was once the home of General Tom Forster who led the doomed Jacobite rebellion in 1715. He was reputed to have hidden in a priest's hole near one of the huge fireplaces before fleeing to France and apparently the ghost of his sister Dorothy still asks guests to take a message to him in exile.

THE TALBOT
OUNDLE, NORTHAMPTONSHIRE

The Talbot occupies an ancient site and before it was substantially rebuilt in 1625 was known as The Tabret. It has macabre links with the past: the stone used for the repairs came from Fotheringay Castle, scene of the execution of Mary Queen of Scots in 1587. The Talbot's main staircase also came from the castle and is the one Mary descended on the way to her death and her ghost is still seen retracing those final steps. Her executioner lodged at the inn the night before he performed his grisly task.

Notwithstanding its past, The Talbot is one of the finest buildings in Oundle, home of the famous public school that was founded in 1556.

THE BUSH INN
MORWENSTOW, CORNWALL

Morwenstow stands just a few hundred yards from the sea at the head of a narrow combe and often feels the full force of Atlantic gales and storms.

The oldest parts of The Bush date from AD 950 when it was a hermit's cell, other sections being added by Cistercian monks in the thirteenth century. These early settlers were well suited to the wild location for they believed such places away from other men to be more holy.

No one is sure of the ghost's identity or from which period of history it comes, but locked doors have mysteriously opened, footsteps heard and shadowy figures seen.

THE WHITE HART
CHALFONT ST PETER, BUCKINGHAMSHIRE

There are two Chalfonts, St Peter and St Giles. The latter is where Milton stayed during an epidemic of the plague to finish *Paradise Lost* and where he wrote *Paradise Regained*. Both villages are just to the north of a glorious section of woodland called Burnham Beeches, which in autumn is transformed into acres of magical colour.

The White Hart in Chalfont St Peter dates back to the mid-eighteenth century and is one of the few pubs that can boast a musical ghost. A nineteenth-century landlord named Donald Ross used to entertain his customers by playing the violin, an activity that he still enjoys.

BUSBY STOOP INN
SANDHUTTON, NORTH YORKSHIRE

A whitewashed inn on a remote crossroads, the Busby Stoop is named after Tom Busby, who was hanged and gibbeted here in 1702. The gallows that bore his rotting body stood opposite the inn and his ghost still patrols the area, his head drooping and the hangman's noose around his neck. He visits the pub from time to time, and the landlord always keeps a chair reserved for him.

Busby's crime was to beat his father-in-law, Daniel Auty, to death with a hammer after a row about money.

The pub today is very popular with racegoers attending Thirsk races a few miles down the road.

KING'S ARMS
ROTHERFIELD, EAST SUSSEX

Rotherfield stands over five hundred feet above sea-level in the Weald, about ten miles south of Tunbridge Wells. The River Rother rises here and meanders along the Kent and Sussex borders down to the coast at Rye.

The King's Arms is a typical Wealden building, half-timbered and hung with red tiles. It was originally part of a brewery and finally became an inn in 1731. There are stories of hauntings and strange happenings at the King's Arms but no one has been able to identify the ghosts that occupy this atmospheric pub.

CASTLE INN
CASTLETON, DERBYSHIRE

Castleton is in the heart of the Peak District and is surrounded by some of the caverns for which the area is famous: Speedwell, Peak and Blue John being the best known. The village is also dominated by the impressive ruins of Peveril Castle, immortalized in Sir Walter Scott's novel, *Peveril of the Peak*.

The seventeenth-century Castle Inn is haunted by a young woman who waits for her wedding breakfast. She was left at the altar and died of a broken heart. It is also said that the body of a woman is buried beneath the entrance to the inn, there being a pagan belief that this would bring good luck to a new building.

Garland Day, a festive occasion with processions and morris dancing, is held on 29 May in Castleton, supposedly to celebrate the Restoration of Charles II.

GREEN TREE
HATFIELD WOODHOUSE, SOUTH YORKSHIRE

This popular pub originated as a simple alehouse in the sixteenth century, parts of the interior still giving an indication of its age. It gradually developed into a posting house on the route north to York, and over the years has been considerably enlarged and modernized.

During the Civil War at the fierce and bloody battle at Marston Moor some thirty miles to the north of Hatfield Woodhouse, four thousand Royalist soldiers were slain in one evening. During that same evening a group of Cavaliers came upon a Roundhead staying at the Green Tree and hung the unfortunate soldier from a beam in his room. His ghost has haunted the pub ever since.

THE BIRDCAGE
THAME, OXFORDSHIRE

Thame is an ancient market town with an exceptionally wide main street almost a mile long. There are several notable old buildings lining both sides of the road, one of which is The Birdcage, a fifteenth-century half-timbered, gabled pub.

It is uncertain how long the building has been in use as licensed premises but certainly no less than a hundred years. It derives its name from previous functions, for many years it was a prison and lock-up. Captured French soldiers were kept here during the Napoleonic Wars and at one time the building was divided, housing prisoners in the cellars and lepers on the top floor. The ghost of one of the lepers has haunted The Birdcage since he was stoned to death by the people of Thame.

THE ANGEL
PETWORTH, WEST SUSSEX

Petworth's narrow streets filled with half-timbered houses wind away from the market-place and its eighteenth-century Town Hall. This small town has grown up outside the gates of Petworth House, which was originally a thirteenth-century manor house, but was largely rebuilt at the end of the seventeenth century. Its magnificent park was laid out in the 1750s by 'Capability' Brown.

The Angel originated in the late fifteenth century when it was of open-plan construction with a hole in the roof for escaping smoke. The huge inglenook fireplace dates from 1600 and is connected with The Angel's ghost, that of a little old grey-haired lady. She was supposedly sitting by the fire waiting for a friend to come downstairs when the friend fell down the stairs and died. The little old lady herself died from shock just two days later, but has apparently remained by the fireplace ever since.

NEW INN
PEMBRIDGE, HEREFORD AND WORCESTER

Originally a farmhouse, this attractive half-timbered building was known for many years as the 'Inn without a name'. Its proximity to Pembridge's open market hall probably led to it becoming an alehouse, since the farmer would have brewed and sold ale to the local wool merchants. By the seventeenth century it had been extended into an inn and also housed the local court for many years.

The New Inn is apparently haunted by two ghosts, one is a young girl who appears only to women, the other a red-coated soldier bearing a sword.

A huge round-backed settle in the bar is said to be part of an old dismantled cockpit and a reminder of coaching days is a whip rack in the public bar.

THE PLOUGH
CLIFTON HAMPDEN, OXFORDSHIRE

The Plough stands in the upper part of Clifton Hampden just above the river Thames and is typical of the many thatched cottages in Oxfordshire. Its thatch is so thick that the roof resembles a tea-cosy.

The village was part of the Hampden family estate. John Hampden, Oliver Cromwell's cousin, was a politician very much involved in the events that preceded the Civil War. When fighting eventually broke out he fought with the Parliamentarians but was killed early in the campaign by Prince Rupert's cavalry.

A room in The Plough is named in Hampden's honour and it is said that his ghost can be heard pacing the floor.

THE OLD INN

WIDECOMBE IN THE MOOR, DEVON

The elegant 120-feet-high granite tower of St Pancras soars above the huddled cottages of Widecombe, a tiny village in the middle of Dartmoor. The church tower was paid for by the prosperous tin miners who had worked the moors since medieval times.

On each second Tuesday in September the village echoes with the sounds of Widecombe Fair, featured in the famous song along with 'Uncle Tom Cobleigh and all'.

The Old Inn certainly lives up to its name having been built as a pub in the fourteenth century. The two bars, with low ceilings and big stone fireplaces, have two ghosts, but about whom little is known. One is of a man called Harry and the other a young girl who could possibly be Mary Jay, an eighteenth-century orphan who hanged herself when she became pregnant by a farm-hand.

OLD SILENT INN

STANBURY, WEST YORKSHIRE

The bleak Haworth moors of the Brontës completely surround this lonely inn, which was originally known as The Eagle, its change of name resulting from an incident involving Bonnie Prince Charlie. In the mid-eighteenth century while the Young Pretender was on the run he stayed at the inn for several weeks, depending on the silence of the locals for his safety and freedom, hence the inn's new name.

One of the inn's nineteenth-century landladies used to feed many of the cats that roamed wild on the hillsides nearby, summoning her pets by ringing a bell from the inn's doorway. People still hear the sound of the bell today and the present landlord claims that an unusually large number of cats still congregate outside the pub on occasions, perhaps drawn by the sound of the ghostly bell.

THE BULL
LONG MELFORD, SUFFOLK

The impressive timbered façade of The Bull was only uncovered in 1935 when its Georgian brick frontage was removed during renovation. Originally built for a rich wool merchant in 1450, The Bull became an inn in 1580.

Impressively carved and moulded timbers fill the interior and on one huge upright is the figure of a 'wodewose', the mythical wild man of the woods that features in Suffolk folk tales.

During the Civil War a local yeoman named Richard Evered was attacked and killed in the entrance hall. His murderer was subsequently hanged and the ghosts of one or both men haunt The Bull. Furniture has moved of its own accord, things have been thrown around and a deathly chill been felt in the dining-room.

BUCKET OF BLOOD
PHILLACK, CORNWALL

Perhaps the most gruesomely titled pub in the country, the Bucket of Blood has a vividly illustrated sign to match its name. Apparently some two hundred years ago the licensee instead of drawing water from the pub's well drew a bucket of blood. It transpired that a headless corpse had been thrown down the well, although it was never discovered who by.

The building, part of which dates back to the twelfth century, is supposedly haunted by a monk, seemingly unconnected with the story surrounding the pub's name. In addition to the ghostly monk there are other signs of haunting: furniture has been seen to move around of its own accord, floorboards to give under the weight of invisible feet and doors to bang on a calm day when the pub was empty.

PHOTOGRAPHIC NOTES

All the photographs in this book were taken with Olympus OM2 cameras using lenses ranging from 24 mm to 200 mm and either Fujichrome 50 ASA or Kodachrome 25 ASA film depending on the weather and light conditions. I find that the Kodak film offers the finest grain for better reproduction but the Fuji has an extra richness in colour, which is especially useful when working in poor light.

One of the main problems I encountered when photographing this selection of English pubs was separating the lovely old buildings from their more modern surroundings, which often spoil a pub's charm. This meant that I had to take many close-up shots for which I used wide-angle lenses and a perspective control lens to correct the converging verticals, although I have deliberately distorted some shots for extra effect. The George and Pilgrim in Glastonbury is a fine fifteenth-century pub that is now, unfortunately, flanked by two modern banks. In this instance I used a telephoto lens to achieve the correct framing and took the shot from a distance, after a patient wait for a gap in the traffic that streamed along the road in front of the pub.

Wherever possible I have tried not to include people and vehicles, as fashions and registration numbers can quickly date photographs, and often detract from the character of a building that has perhaps remained unchanged for several hundred years. Possibly the greatest unavoidable problem with photographing buildings is the presence of television aerials, telephone wires, power cables and incongruous modern signs, which unfortunately have to be accepted as part of the contemporary landscape. Shooting times were usually restricted to early morning and mid-afternoon to avoid the inclusion of customers' cars during opening hours.

Photographing some of the waterside pubs presented the problem of where to take the picture from to get the best angle, as most of them either faced out to sea or on to a river. Remote riverside pubs such as the Golden Ball in Lancashire, involved making a long trek along the opposite river bank to get directly opposite the building.

When photographing the haunted pubs I tried to use natural lighting to create an appropriate atmosphere, augmented by graduated filters to darken or colour the sky.

BIBLIOGRAPHY

Batchelor, Denzil *The English Inn*, Batsford, 1963; U.S.A. Hastings House, 1963

Bottomley, Frank *The Inn Explorer's Guide*, Kaye and Ward, 1984; U.S.A. David & Charles, 1984

Brander, Michael *The Life and Sport of the Inn*, Gentry Books, 1973

Bruning, Ted and Paulin, Keith *Historic English Inns*, David & Charles, 1982

Burke, John *The English Inn*, Batsford, 1981; U.S.A. Holmes & Meier, 1981

The Good Beer Guide, CAMRA, (Published annually)

The Good Pub Guide, Consumers Association and Hodder & Stoughton, (Published annually)

Coysh, A. W. *Historic English Inns*, David & Charles, 1972; U.S.A. Drake Publications, 1972

Hogg, Garry *The English Country Inn*, Batsford, 1981

Pevsner, Nikolaus *The Buildings of England* (Series), Penguin

Richardson, A. E. *The Old Inns of England*, Batsford, 1934; U.S.A. Charles Scribner's Sons, 1934

INDEX